# THE THREE RIMBAUDS

THE FRENCH LIST

Dominique Noguez

# THE THREE RIMBAUDS

TRANSLATED BY SETH WHIDDEN

LONDON NEW YORK CALCUTTA

www.bibliofrance.in

This work is published with the support of the
Publication Assistance Programmes of the Institut français

Seagull Books, 2022

First published in French as *Les Trois Rimbaud*
by Dominique Noguez
© Les Éditions de Minuit, Paris, 1986

First published in English by Seagull Books, 2022
English Translation and Notes © Seth Whidden, 2022

ISBN  978 0 8574 2 882 0

British Library Cataloguing-in-Publication Data
A catalogue record for this book is available from
the British Library

Typeset by Seagull Books, Calcutta, India
Printed and bound in the USA by Integrated Books International

# CONTENTS

By this, and this only, have we existed
Which is not to be found in our obituaries
T. S. Eliot, *The Wasteland*

When Cardinal Richelieu drew up the idea for the Académie française in 1635, he decided that its forty members should have lifetime membership. So important are *les immortels* that their contribution to the French language endures long after they pass away, long after a successor takes their place. When poet Arthur Rimbaud was elected to his seat in 1930, fellow poet and academician Paul Valéry gave the speech to welcome him. While the election was meant to honour Rimbaud's entire body of work, Valéry conceded that most would feel that Rimbaud had been elected because of the literary works written after his return from Africa, which had received such tremendous critical acclaim: *African Nights* and *The Black Gospel*. For Valéry, reading him in this way was not seeing the whole picture, and the occasion of Rimbaud's election to the

Académie was an opportunity to look beyond the major works of that period, to reconsider his earlier ones that were all but forgotten.

Except that he wasn't elected, and they were far from forgotten. When Rimbaud returned from Africa in March 1891 he didn't go back to literature but, rather, to the hospital, to have part of his leg amputated and to recover, and then, after a brief convalescence and one last attempt to leave Europe, he died in Marseille on 10 November of that year. Works like *African Nights*, *L.*, *The Black Gospel*, or even the unfinished *System of Modern Life* were never even imagined let alone written,[1] and the Académie never considered Rimbaud for one of their prestigious seats.[2] In 1930, even without a speech from Valéry, Rimbaud criticism was gaining momentum, with forty years of commentary under its belt and many more studies still to come. Without ever having been an academician, though, Rimbaud continues to

---

1 Not by Rimbaud, anyway; Noguez's *Amour noir* (Gallimard, 1997) featured the character Laetitia, frequently written in the novel as 'Læ' or 'L.'

2 As for Rimbaud, he had a very different Académie in his sights, as he wrote to his friend Ernest Delahaye in June 1872: 'Long live the Academy of Absomphe, despite the waiters' foul moods. It is the most delicate, the most tremulous of garments, the drunkenness induced by virtue of that glacial sage, absomphe. And, afterwards, to sleep in our shit!'—translated from Arthur Rimbaud, *Œuvres complètes* (André Guyaux and Aurélia Cervoni eds) (Paris: Gallimard, 'Bibliothèque de la Pléiade', 2009), pp. 368–9.

benefit from literary immortality thanks to those early works that, written before he turned twenty-one, have never been forgotten. To the contrary, verse poems such as 'The Drunken Boat' and the prose collections *A Season in Hell* and *Illuminations* are among the most important and enduring pieces of modern French poetry for the indelible marks they left while Rimbaud tore through centuries of rules of French verse and thumbed his nose at every authority figure along the way.[3] To this day, French schoolchildren learn to recite poems like 'The Sleeper in the Valley' from memory. 'The Drunken Boat' is painted on a wall in the rue Férou in Paris, near where Rimbaud first recited it to the amazement of his fellow poets in late 1871. The volumes *A Season in Hell* and *Illuminations* continue to baffle critics today for their complexity: obscure and utopian one minute, acutely parodic the next, alternating between biting social and political criticism and delirium to regret and the repudiation of an earlier poetic project.

The autobiographical tones that resonate in critics' ears endure because Rimbaud's lasting, immortal presence in French letters also comes from his life: he was

---

3 Noguez knew full well the importance of these two publications, for he produced a critical edition of them. He opened his foreword by calling them the 'two of the greatest texts of all literatures, of those texts that may be enough for nearly a lifetime'—translated from Dominique Noguez, 'Cris et éblouissements' in Arthur Rimbaud, *Une saison en enfer et Illuminations suivies d'un choix de lettres* (Dominique Noguez ed.) (Paris: La Différence, 'Orphée', 1991), p. 7.

as daring and irreverent in his actions as he was in his poetry, and his life and work have proven irresistible to literary critics, biographers and anyone who has ever been a teenager. Fellow poet Stephane Mallarmé referred to Rimbaud as having had the brilliance of a meteor: while Mallarmé was referring to how a meteor shoots across the sky and burns out just as quickly, Rimbaud's dazzling presence is also the kind of brilliance that demands our attention: we can't help but stare a bit, it's hard to look away.[4]

Like many others, Dominique Noguez (1942–2019) was drawn to such a sight. As a renowned scholar of contemporary cinema, aesthetics and literature in university posts in Montreal and Paris, he had already proven his keen eye for other kinds of brilliance. While most Rimbaud critics of the 1950s, 1960s and 1970s obsessively pursued one or both of the two Rimbauds— the precocious European poet or the African explorer, trader and gunrunner—Noguez had a different take. In the first of a series that he entitled 'More or Less Scholarly Studies' (*Études plus ou moins sçavantes*), he mocked the two dominant approaches in the overly zealous world of literary criticism (what Svetlana Boym

---

4 In this respect Rimbaud is indeed a worthy successor to the mantel of modern poet first defined and embodied by Baudelaire: 'And as they see, they are seen: the vision, the epiphany, flows both ways. In the midst of great spaces, under the bright lights, there is no way to look away'—Marshall Berman, *All That Is Solid Melts into Air: The Experience of Modernity* (London: Verso, 1983), p. 153.

called 'on the one hand, a close, textual, often decon-
structive, reading of the poems and, on the other hand,
evidence of the reemerging interest in Rimbaud's biography and existential experiences'—*Death in Quotation
Marks*, p. 114) by concocting a literary and biographical
study that combined erudition with fabrication, pastiche, parody and irony.[5]

In a 1993 essay, Noguez reflected on the ideas that
had led to *Three Rimbauds*. First and foremost, he
explained, was the pleasure that every child enjoys:
having fun by playing make-believe. The famous
endings to stories from military or political history that
would fascinate him as a child—what would have
happened if Robespierre had been victorious on 9
Thermidor, or Napoleon hadn't been defeated at
Waterloo, or Montcalm in Quebec—became, with age,
similar 'what ifs' about literary history.[6] Acknowledging

---

5 From an interview with Marius Creati. Noguez's blend of elements
that are larger than life and ironic recalls Baudelaire's statement, from
*Fusées*: 'Two fundamental qualities of literature: the supernatural and
irony. A single wink, an aspect in which these two things stand before
the writer, then a Satanic turn of mind. The supernatural includes
local colour and accent: that is to say, intensity, sonority, limpidity,
vibration, depth, and resonance in space and in time'—translated from
Charles Baudelaire, *Œuvres complètes*, VOL. 1 (Claude Pichois ed.)
(Paris: Gallimard, 'Bibliothèque de la Pléiade', 1975), p. 658.

6 Noguez would return to this recurring theme in *L'Interruption*, published the year before his death: 'It seems that you imagine the defeat
of the Greeks at the battle of Salamis.—Yes, it would have been
enough for Themistocles not to be listened to . . . This is just one

his own inability to take things seriously (at least not completely), he wanted to parody texts of literary criticism that tended towards arrogance, in a sub-genre he baptized 'critique-fiction' or 'playful erudition'. The very nature of pastiche—his third reason—is ample justification for the rigour that it requires: when done right, by virtue of adopting the traits and manners of its object, the text reaches the highest level of applied stylistics, psychoanalysis, politics and every dimension of content and tone. In this respect, Noguez took his place in a long history of pastiches of Rimbaud, beginning with his contemporaries: fellow poets who met in the aftermath of the 1871 Paris Commune, filling their *Album zutique* with pastiches, mockeries and other bawdy imitations and jokes. The texts are as lewd as they are examples of literary brio.

Writing the pastiche of a known body of literature is one thing; *pastiching in anticipation*—that is, pastiching an *œuvre* not yet written (or, more accurately, never written at all)—is a very different matter. To make it work, Noguez imagined a Rimbaud returning to a more conventional, classical literary style in the more mature

---

example among many. I also imagine what would have happened if Robespierre had convinced the Convention the day before 9th Thermidor or if, in the 1930s, Colonel de Gaulle had managed to equip the French army with powerful armored divisions. Or if the French, in May 1945, had not drowned the Sétif outbreak in blood'—translated from Dominique Noguez, *L'Interruption* (Paris: Flammarion, 2018), pp. 125–6.

works that he invented for his subject. As he explained, 'Showing what a writer could plausibly have become and what he could have written is also making a statement about who he was, and about the meaning of what he wrote'.[7] The remaining two reasons for this book were aesthetic, the first musical: in response to earlier biographical work that followed the *allegro con brio* of the poet's Parisian period with an *adagio assai* of his time in Harar, Noguez was compelled to complement the two movements of this Rimbaud life-concerto with a third one, a *rondo vivace*.[8] And, finally—crucially—as a reminder that a life can be coherent even with sudden changes of tempo.

And yet, for all its farce, *The Three Rimbauds* remains grounded in reality: Noguez takes a few key moments in Rimbaud's life—carefully, surgically—and turns them sideways, leading the reader through familiar territory only to (with a wink) pull the rug out from underfoot and create a new path for his narrative. To take but one example: the 1888 forgeries that were published in *Le Décadent* were, in Noguez's tale, really poems by Rimbaud: Verlaine recanted his initial claims of forgery and the poems marked the beginning of

---

7 Translated from Dominique Noguez, 'Ressusciter Rimbaud' in *Rimbaud* (Dominique Noguez, Jean Larose and Gilles Marcotte eds) (Paris: Le Castor astral, L'atelier des modernes, 1993), pp. 107–37; here, p. 114.

8 Noguez, 'Ressusciter Rimbaud', pp. 115–16.

Rimbaud's return to the literary world.[9] By splitting
what had previously thought of as two Rimbauds into
three[10]—by adding to the young poet and the African
trader an imagined election of Rimbaud-the-catholic-
patriarch-of-Charleville to the Académie française for
the African works that were never written, years after a
break with the Surrealists and a correspondence with
Thomas Mann, neither of which ever occurred—
Noguez shows that critics' divisions and their related
quest for a unifying narrative to tie them together are
fools' errands. A life, like a body of work, is a messy
affair, neither divisible neatly into discrete movements
nor obediently linear. Bucking the tendency of criticism

9 There is a long tradition of texts, ephemera and photographs by or
of—or claimed to be by or of—Rimbaud; see Seth Whidden, *Arthur
Rimbaud* (London: Reaktion Books, 'Critical Lives', 2018), pp. 159,
182, 184–5.

10 Or four; the precise number is irrelevant. Noguez returned to this
theme at the end of his critical edition of *Une saison en enfer* and
*Illuminations*, saying that the collections: '[P]rove that there are at
least two great movements in Rimbaud's prose, just as critics distin-
guished two great movements in his poetry: complicated, virtuoso,
with rare words (in "The Drunken Boat"), or on the contrary, simple
and musical like a "stupid chorus", a "naive rhythm" (in "Oh seasons,
oh castles"). There will be a third one: the dry, travel notes from Harar
or Ogadine. And a fourth, without words—a way to explore space
after consciousness, to write with the prose of deeds, of walks in the
desert, and of life.'—translated from Dominique Noguez, 'Cris et
éblouissements', p. 21. For his mention of the movements in
Rimbaud's poetry, Noguez refers to Jean-Luc Steinmetz, 'Le Livre
du passage', preface to Steinmetz's edition of Rimbaud's *Œuvres*,
VOL. 2 (Paris: Flammarion, 1989), pp. 9–12.

to make sense of the noise and draw order out of chaos, Noguez's text delightfully riddles the traditional scholarly narrative with holes and then fills them with an epoxy of his own concoction. As Svetlana Boym explains, what results is that:

> Noguez's *Les Trois Rimbaud*, a reduction to absurdity of the obsessions of contemporary critics, is a rewriting of Borges' ironic scholarly essays on Pierre Menard. It is another exercise in implausible criticism, another reduction to absurdity of the critical enterprise. At the same time, it provides a powerful insight into not only the institution of literature but also the institutions of contemporary criticism, which would happily proliferate Rimbauds and kill and resurrect authors as long as that helps to strengthen the critic's identity and authority.
>
> (*Death in Quotation Marks*, p. 116)

Boym's comparison to Borges' essay 'Pierre Menard, Author of the Quixote' (1939) is entirely apposite, and Noguez openly acknowledged his debt to Borges: for his blended tone of serious literary study and humorous irony, raising questions of literary authority and interpretation along the way. Like Borges simultaneously fabricating and complicating Menard, Noguez offers an essay of Rimbaud that, for all its fantasy, touches bedrock: from this death of the author rises a fresh, new consideration of *vie* and *œuvre*, both revalorized for all their messiness. After witnessing decades of obsessive, reductive and smothering literary and biographical criticism—what he refers to as a paranoid or delirious tendency, practiced by 'ultratextualists' who see meaning in everything[11]—Noguez shows the reader how not to lose the forest for the trees: by mocking the possibility of a coherent narrative that accounts fully for a life or a work, his pastiche revels in all of the dimensions that provide complexity and richness. Revealing the many layers that don't fit together perfectly (and sometimes even contradict each other), he reminds us of what is truly important in a life: the joy that exists whether or not things make sense—and especially when they don't. As he explained in an interview, 'there is nothing greater, no finer pleasure than in the music of a text, a satire's caustic nature, and invention worthy of fiction'.[12] Such is what he hoped for the story he tells in *The Three Rimbauds*: 'that in the end we almost believe it'.[13]

In 2017, the Académie française awarded Noguez its 'prix d'académie' for the entirety of his work. With this recognition, the Académie bestowed upon him its motto: 'À l'immortalité'. While it never offered a place

---

11 Noguez, 'Ressusciter Rimbaud', pp. 122–3.

12 Translated from an interview with Charles Patin O'Coohoon.

13 Translated from an interview with Charles Patin O'Coohoon.

to Arthur Rimbaud, it rendered immortal the questions that underpin poetry, life and the improbable combination of erudition and imagination that bestow upon literature its brilliance: the brightest meteor against the darkest sky.

\*

### A Note on the Text

To best appreciate the unique blend of erudition and invention in *The Three Rimbauds*, all footnotes accompanying the text are from the original. It would be nearly impossible for the reader to be familiar with every minute detail of literary history to which the text refers, nor the degree (or lack) of veracity or the context for every reference—whether 'quoted' by Noguez or not; as one reviewer put it, 'there isn't a single detail that is not a wink, not one whose humour fails to enchant'.[14] Shedding light on many of the winks, my own notes follow Noguez's text in a separate section at the end of this volume. In this way, *The Three Rimbauds* is not laden with additional symbols and readers are able to appreciate it in English—with its real and faux scholarship, its delicate balance of (real and invented) scholarly acumen and literary flair—just as in the French original.

---

14 Translated from A. R., 'Le faussaire inspiré', *L'Express* (11–17 April 1986).

## BIBLIOGRAPHY

A. R. 'Le faussaire inspiré', *L'Express* (11–17 April 1986).

BOYER-WEINMANN, Martine. *La Relation biographique: enjeux contemporains*. Seyssel: Éditions Champ Vallon, 'Détours', 2005.

BOYM, Svetlana. *Death in Quotation Marks: Cultural Myths of the Modern Poet*. Cambridge, MA: Harvard University Press, 1991.

CERQUIGLINI, Blanche. 'Quand la vie est un roman: les biographies romanesques', *Le Débat* 165(3) (2011): 146–57.

CREATI, Marius. 'Entretien avec Dominique Noguez', *La Promenade: BlogZine di Cultura* (8 May 2010). Available at: https://bit.ly/3yFSUpI (last accessed on 9 August 2021).

DION, Robert. 'Un discours perturbé: la fiction dans le biographique' in Robert Dion, Frances Fortier, Barbara Havercroft and Hans-Jürgen Lüsebrink (eds), *Vies en récit: formes littéraires et médiatiques de la biographie et de l'autobiographie*. Québec: Éditions Nota Bene, 'Convergences No. 38', 2007, pp. 279–99.

—— and Frances Fortier. *Écrire l'écrivain: formes contemporaines de la vie d'auteur*. Montréal: Presses de l'Université de Montréal, 'Espace littéraire', 2010.

—— and Mahigan Lepage. 'L'archive du biographe'. *Protée* 35(3): 11–21.

JEANDILLOU, Jean-François. 'La "fiction où tout est vrai"'. *Poétique* 176(2) (2014): 211–19.

LÉON, Paul. 'L'écrivain et ses images, le paratexte pho-
tographique' in Jean-Pierre Montier, Liliane Louvel,
Danièle Méaux and Philippe Ortel (eds), *Littérature et
photographie*. Rennes: Presses universitaires de Rennes,
'Interférences', 2008, pp. 113–26.

LIS, Jerzy. 'Pour une biographie imaginaire d'Arthur
Rimbaud'. *Lublin Studies in Modern Languages and
Literature* 38(1) (2014): 39–51. Available at: https://-
bit.ly/37wBEXP (last accessed on 9 August 2021).

O'COOHOON, Charles Patin. 'La vérité selon Dominique',
*Zone Littéraire* (3 July 2006). Available at: https://-
bit.ly/3jAyKXy (last accessed on 9 August 2021).

REMILLIEUX, Daniel. 'Rimbaud, la mémoire incertaine et
la postérité'. *Parade sauvage* 19 (December 2003):
206–20.

SAINT-AMAND, Denis. 'Anomie de Rimbaud' in Pascal
Brissette and Marie-Pier Luneau (eds), *Deux siècles de
malédiction littéraire*. Liège: Presses universitaires de
Liège, 2014, pp. 121–35.

WHIDDEN, Seth. *Arthur Rimbaud*. London: Reaktion
Books, 'Critical Lives', 2018.

### RELATED WORKS BY DOMINIQUE NOGUEZ

NOGUEZ, Dominique. *Le Grantécrivain & autres textes*.
Paris, Gallimard, 2000.

———. *L'Interruption*. Paris, Flammarion, 2018.

———. Cris et éblouissements' in Arthur Rimbaud, *Une saison en enfer et Illuminations suivies d'un choix de lettres*

(Dominique Noguez ed.). Paris: La Différence, 'Orphée', 1991, pp. 7–22. Reprinted by Éditions du Sandre, 2010.

———. 'Ressusciter Rimbaud' in Dominique Noguez, Jean Larose and Gilles Marcotte (eds), *Rimbaud*. Paris: Le Castor astral, 'L'atelier des modernes', 1993, pp. 107–37.

———. 'Le jour où Lautréamont a rencontré Rimbaud'. *Cahiers Lautréamont* 81–84 (2007): 20–33.


THE SERIES 'ÉTUDES PLUS OU MOINS SÇAVANTES'

NOGUEZ, Dominique. *Les Trois Rimbaud*. Paris: Éditions de Minuit, 1986.

———. *Lénine dada*. Paris: Robert Laffont, 1989. The second edition was published by Le Dilettante in 2007.

———. *Sémiologie du parapluie et autres textes*. Paris: La Différence, 1990.

———. *La Véritable Histoire du football & autres révélations*. Paris: Gallimard, 2006.

———. *Montaigne au bordel & autres surprises*. Paris: Maurice Nadeau, 2010.

THE THREE RIMBAUDS

When Arthur Rimbaud was inducted into the Académie française on 16 January 1930, no one seemed to remember the 'man with the soles of wind', the diabolical cherub from 'Nina's Replies' and 'The Seated Man', or the Seer thug who had dominated the headlines in the little world of French poetry in 1872. Curiously enough, Paul Valéry, whose speech officially welcomed the new academician and who was known for being more meticulous (in his foreword to La Fontaine or Mallarmé, for example), made quick work of Rimbaud's early works and dispatched them in three quick sentences:

> I haven't forgotten, dear Sir, that you didn't take your first steps among us with this large tome [*African Nights*]: it was preceded by a number of small chapbooks, which ought to be republished, someday. In them, you show that you are, in verse as in prose, one of our first Symbolists: a little less well known than the others but a little more precocious; a little more tormented and a little more visionary. Specifically, before living your thousand and one nights in Africa, you had had the luxury of a brief 'Night

of Hell', and he who would later travel the world on so many sailboats and cargo ships imagined himself a 'drunken boat' . . .

More than a half-century later, everything is happening as if the critics were suffering from the same amnesia and as if, just as for the exegesis of *The Black Gospel* or *Looking Without Eyes*, they forgot that these works had been preceded by texts entitled *A Season in Hell* or *Illuminations*, and that there is perhaps good reason to exhume these early works, against which to better measure the more mature ones.

Furthermore, this orthodoxy is nothing new. Let us not forget that it goes back to André Breton and the Surrealists: during the brief period which separates the first *Manifesto* from the disputes of May 1925, when Rimbaud distances himself from Breton's *Address to the Pope* (in which, ironically, Rimbaud is quoted . . . ).[1] It is when Aragon and Breton—as everyone knows, authors of admiring pastiches of *Illuminations* going back to 1918 (in the journal *Les Trois Roses*, published in Grenoble)—repeatedly highlight the continuity between the texts of 1870–1875 and the sonnets of 1886–1888 or the 'Futurist' prose of 1899–1910, and even the 1893 novel. As Aragon notes in *Libertinage* (1924):

1 'Nous ne sommes pas au monde', *La Révolution surréaliste* 3 (15 April 1925).

Poems like *Instrumentation*, *Doctrine* or *Omega* are all similarly the fruits of the visionary of *The Drunken Boat* and *Illuminations*: through them it is possible to trace the path he took. With *Doctrine*, the poet stopped fleeing into the wandering and the black light of his poetic project of *seeing*. He makes a break with a lucidity that is sarcastic while remaining serene:

> So that the poet may be
> Surrounded by love, when he sits
> Under the pilasters
> Of the white crypt where the incense
> Rises in lactose flakes
> Among the stars

And, in the 1924 *Manifesto*, while giving examples of Surrealist images, Breton doesn't hesitate to precede the famous example of *African Nights* (the only 'novel' to escape his condemnation, perhaps because with its photographs it paves the way for *Nadja*) with a quotation from *Illuminations*:

And here are some examples, in order:

*Lovers' feasts ring out over the canals suspended behind the chalets. The hunting of chimes clamours in the gorges.*—Arthur Rimbaud.

*The syringes of blood of the night.*—Arthur Rimbaud.

Even in the leaflet that consummates the break-up between the author of *African Nights* and the Surrealist movement, the first Rimbaud is not forgotten. One could even say that he is mobilized against the later one, the one who dares to 'urge Monsieur Breton not to put his name at the bottom of the ridiculous "Open letter to Monsieur Paul Claudel, Ambassador of France in Japan",'[2] the one whom Aragon, in an about-turn which would soon be customary for him, henceforth calls a 'bazaar adventurer' and 'defrocked genius'[3]:

> And let us not be made to believe that there was some fatality in what some of us, with residual indulgence for the unsurpassable poet, the *mouth of light*, of *Illuminations*, are still tempted to hold for a transient failure. In truth, on the razor's edge, the high-wire walker chose to fall. The duvet-covered bed of *African Nights*, where we already felt that there were too many feathers, was not enough for the tired vagabond. Now—denying the 'I have never been Christian' of this *Season in Hell* which, let's be honest, only lasted a season—he needs to wallow, like a vulgar Paul Claudel, in the abject *bosom* of Catholicism. The right to contradict oneself, I know, but honestly! M. Rimbaud had

---

2 Letter-tract dated 1 July 1925.
3 *Les Nouvelles littéraires*, 18 July 1925.

indeed *seen*: 'That would be the French way of life, the path of honour.' He is there.

This stark way of seeing things would be constant for Breton (very likely the author of the tract). Still in 1939, barely two years after the poet's death and despite the reconciliation between them in 1935, he writes, in *Anthology of Black Humour*:

> Rimbaud therefore had two lives. We will ignore the second—in which the puppet took over, in which a pathetic clown, transformed somewhat belatedly into an academician and who escaped the Nobel Prize by the slimmest of margins,[4] makes his money belt and his Virgin's medals ring out for all to hear—and consider only the Rimbaud of 1871–1872, a veritable god of puberty, the likes of which no mythologies had ever seen.

Another fervent reader of Rimbaud making the connection between *Illuminations* and the rest of his work is Jean Cocteau who, after having recalled in 1925, 'We are living in Galeries Lafayette Ducasse-Rimbaud,' greets the release of *The Black Gospel* (1928) in these terms:

> This book teaches the new anarchy of loving God without limits, of enabling prudence up to

---

4 There was indeed talk of Rimbaud for the 1937 Nobel Prize in the weeks before his death.

the point of reason itself. The man with the soles of wind has stopped, but not to seek shelter. He is exposing himself to another storm. His illuminations become brighter without being any less unbearable. It's the same lightning. *The Black Gospel* is a season in purgatory, which is more inhuman than Hell because no one burns there. It's no longer the African night with its syringes of blood. It's a sleepless night. But in this night we catch a glimmer of hope. And, still, genius.[5]

Equally distanced from two attitudes that oppose each other but converge in their degree of bias—ignoring or concealing the first Rimbaud, which is practically traditional, and, inversely and following Breton, celebrating it exclusively (due to his animosity towards the second Rimbaud)—Cocteau is the only one who gave equal weight to the two periods of his work.

Such is the example that we wish to pursue in this study, persuaded that we will read each of the two groups of texts better (for now, let us accept that it is necessary to see them as two distinct entities) by rereading them in this way. The first ones, often considered obscure, are illuminated by the second ones; and the latter ones, while more famous and more highly regarded, are no less enriched by the confrontation with the earlier ones. To put it simply, and before attempting to develop any specific examples, leaving for future study

---

5 'Un génie au purgatoire', *Le Figaro*, 17 February 1928.

the task of considering more fully this unavoidable confrontation, the first problem remains: that of the legitimacy of the expressions 'first' and 'second' Rimbaud with which we find ourselves confronted, without having discussed that legitimacy directly yet.

## Two or Three Rimbauds?

If, for Breton and as we have seen, it stems from obvious polemical reasons, the distinction between two Rimbauds is often adopted by Rimbaud scholars or critics unaware of its underlying hostility towards the writer. It would be enough to cite Victor Segalen ('Le Double Rimbaud' in *Mercure de France*, 15 April 1906), Jean-Marie Carré (*Les Deux Rimbaud*, 1928) or Hugo Ball (*Die Flucht aus der Zeit*, 1946). What is frustrating is that we never truly know in which realm we should be: in his work or in his life. Certainly, as we are dealing with a man for whom the two are so inextricably linked, at least until *The Black Gospel*, conflating the two might seem justified without raising cries of Lansonism. There is one major weakness, however: it blinds us to the fact that the expression is doubly inappropriate. Because if, in terms of his life, it is legitimate to make such clean breaks, then we shouldn't only distinguish between only two Rimbauds. As far as his work is considered—as we hope to show convincingly later in this study—there is but one.

But, first, his life. Breton's formulas are too imprecise for us to know if for him the second Rimbaud, the one he doesn't like (at least the one he no longer likes after their break-up) begins in 1875, when the poet begins his long period of wandering outside of France, or in 1893, when he resurfaces, and with brilliance, in the Parisian literary world captivated by his *African Nights*. It's worth mentioning that the only date Breton gives is 1871–1872, which would seem to indicate that for him, 'good' Rimbaud's work ends before *A Season in Hell* (dated 'April–August 1873') and *Illuminations* (for the most part completed in 1874, and given to Verlaine in February 1875). This restriction is all the more ridiculous because Breton then proceeds to include, in his *Anthology*, Rimbaud's letter to Ernest Delahaye from 14 October 1875 . . . but we shall leave that for now. Instead, we note that it is 1893 (or, at the very earliest, 1891, the year of his secret return to Paris) that most Rimbaud scholars generally choose for the beginning of the 'second' Rimbaud. On that point it is hard to agree with them: 1875 is no less decisive than other periods into which his life can be categorized. It may be a matter of a few months, if not a year or two: Antoine Adam—despite too often being uncertain—was able to plausibly date 'Devotion' and 'Democracy', from *Illuminations*, to 1876 (which makes one think, as Suzanne Bernard does, that they were not included in the poems given to Verlaine in Stuttgart and were only added to them after the fact). Either way, whether 1875 or 1876, it was at this time that the poet's silence began, a silence scarcely interrupted by the five sonnets sent to *Le Décadent* in 1888 (the untitled sonnet published in 1886 was clearly apocryphal)[6] and which would continue until 1893. 1875 or 1876: it was at this time that the interminable series of travelling and exploring began, leading him to Aden and Harar, and inspiring *African Nights*. If there's nothing to suggest that the idea for the book came to him as early as 1875–1876, it would be similarly inappropriate to put the idea in his head and for it to take shape merely at the moment when he returns incognito to Paris to settle down: two of his acquaintances from his travelling period, Armand Savouré, on the subject of autumn 1888, and Alfred Bardey both confirm that he wrote a great deal in Africa.[7] The travel notes plundered by Henri Donbiville corroborate the fact that, while we don't have the book's framework, its idea—which we could even call its haunting—and its numerous detailed descriptions that have been reprinted verbatim were mostly from before 1891.

---

6 'It splendours under the blue of athletic Natures.' On this, see Noël Richard, *Le Mouvement décadent* (Paris: Nizet, 1968), pp. 201–02.

7 Savouré: 'He put me up for a month. A pretty decent unfurnished house. I could only sleep on my travelling cot, and, for the month I was there, I never figured out where he slept, as I saw him day and night writing at a crummy table' (Letter to Georges Maurevert, 1930?). Bardey: 'I think that he was still writing [. . .] and I [. . .] had the feeling that, after making enough money, Rimbaud was preparing a return to the literary world.' (Letter to Paterne Berrichon, 16 July 1897, *Mercure de France* [15 May–16 June 1939]: 19).

N° 2. 3ᵉ An. (2ᵉ Série.)                    1-15 Janvier 1888

LE

# DÉCADENT

REVUE LITTÉRAIRE BI-MENSUELLE

Directeur : ANATOLE BAJU

PRIX : QUINZE CENTIMES

## SOMMAIRE

## BUREAUX

54, BOULEVARD DE LA CHAPELLE, 54

Dépôt central chez L. Vanier, 19, quai Saint-Michel

PARIS

Cover page of the journal *Le Décadent* (January 1888) where Rimbaud is published.

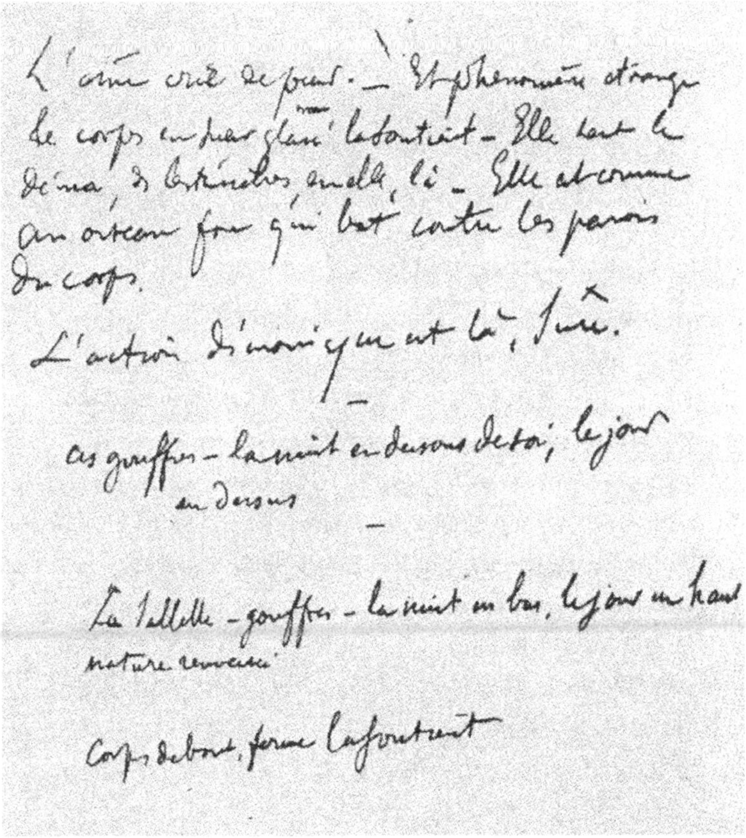

A page from the manuscript of *The Black Gospel* (1925).

In our opinion, the interruption that 1891 represents is significantly less important. To be sure, the traveller —could one say the runaway?—returns home, and homecomings are always charged with meaning. There's no doubt that he closes himself up in a rue Visconti mansard to write his masterpiece, and this retreat was not nothing. But we could legitimately consider that it is merely the result of what he had decided (?) sixteen years earlier when he went to Germany, then to Italy, to Austria and Holland, to Java, to Sweden and to Denmark, before making it to Alexandria, Cyprus, and then the Arabian peninsula. Let us not forget that, if he was no longer considered dead (as had been the case in 1889) and if it was merely a question of rhetorical flourish when Gustave Kahn deplored to the journalist Jules Huret in 1891 that Rimbaud was 'forgotten',[8] for most of his former Parisian acquaintances the news of his return would only break in February 1893, when, with enthusiasm and after a sleepless night of fervent reading, Alfred Vallette decided to publish *African Nights* with the Mercure de France (the manuscript had been discreetly left at 15 rue de l'Échaudé-Saint-Germain, where he was living and which still houses the publisher's offices). The only ones who knew were Rimbaud's friend Ernest Delahaye and his sister Isabelle, who was far from Paris. It is certainly shocking to think that, living in the rue

---

8  Jules Huret, *Enquête sur l'évolution littéraire* (Paris: Thôt, 1982[1891]), p. 327.

Visconti, in the heart of literary Paris, Rimbaud was able
to stay incognito from his return in July 1891 to the start
of 1893—that is, more than a year and a half—and that
he could have dined in the rue Monsieur-le-Prince or
even walked around the Luxembourg Gardens[9] without
ever bumping into Verlaine, for example, who haunted
the quartier.[10] But, as the famous photo from 1892
attests, with his gaunt frame, his beard and his cropped
grey hair, even if they had seen him, he would have
been practically unrecognizable to those who had
known him as a teenager. That impression is confirmed
by Léautaud's retrospective account in which he evokes,
upon the writer's death, their first meeting, in 1893:

> In the afternoon, around five o'clock, I leave the
> Mercure to go to the rue Dauphine to buy liver
> for Blanchou, the cat. Miss Naudy had put the
> newspaper on my desk. However, on the way to
> the shop, I stop at the newsagent in front of the
> Odeon and look at some of the papers. *Paris-
> Soir*, which I have not looked at for a long time
> [. . .], is in front of me. Instinctively, I open it. On
> the first page I see a title: ARTHUR RIMBAUD. I
> immediately think that it must be an article about
> Rimbaud. I start looking at it, I read the begin-
> ning: Arthur Rimbaud has just died. Buzzing

9 See the letters to Ernest Delahaye from 10 September and 25
October 1892.

10 'I met him at his regular cafe, the *François Premier*, boulevard
Saint-Michel' (said Jules Huret, *Enquête*, p. 81).

with surprise and impatience, I can no longer stay
still. I plunk down twenty-five cents, run to the
butcher to buy the liver, and race back. Nothing
was happening quickly enough. Rimbaud dead!
He, who, just three months earlier, was speaking
to me, so alert, so full of enthusiasm and pro-
jects. [. . .] Duhamel arrives: 'Have you seen
*L'Écho de Paris*?,' he asks me. I say no. 'They're
describing Rimbaud as if he were a Gallimard
author!' I tell him, 'That's leaving out three-
quarters of his life!' He is thinking about writing
a letter to the editor. And we begin talking
about the deceased, me reminiscing about the
first time that I saw him, even before he came
to Mercure, one day, with Van Bever. At the
time I was working for the glove-maker Berr
where my father had got me a job as a 'gallery
assistant'. Around seven o'clock, I had gone
to meet Van Bever in the rue Monsieur-le-
Prince to go have dinner. We were on the rue
de l'Ancienne-Comédie when coming right
towards us was a man, around forty years old,
thin, rather tall, balding with very short grey
hair, thick beard, high cheekbones, and eyes of
the clearest blue you've ever seen: one of those
hermit faces that I find so fascinating to look at,
walking with long strides, a book in his hand.
Van Bever gently elbows me and says, 'That's
Rimbaud. Did you hear? He's back.' Vallette

had tipped Van Bever off that very morning. I hadn't even heard of Rimbaud at that point, I think . . .[11]

However, even in early 1893, Rimbaud is far from an unknown in literary circles, at least in the ones with journals that are considered 'Symbolist' or 'Decadent'. The poems that he had sent to the *Décadent* in 1888 made some noise, particularly because of Verlaine's initial objections and claims that they were forgeries.[12] At any rate, they lead us to believe that on this score, too, there was no major interruption in 1891–1893 and Rimbaud's decision to restart his literary activities took place well before the publication of *African Nights*. There is no interruption afterwards, either: despite his success, the prodigal son will take a long time to change his habits, remaining on the margins of the literary world (invited to participate in the Académie Goncourt in 1896, he refuses almost indignantly), only leaving his semi-reclusion in the rue Visconti for trips outside of

---

11 *Journal littéraire* 11 (26 January 1937).

12 'As for the 'sonnets' published in the *Décadent*, I declare that they were not written by this poet' (Letter from Verlaine to Cazals, 8 October 1888, published in *La Cravache parisienne* [11 October 1888]). Verlaine persists in a letter to Jules Christophe (1 November 1888), also published in the *Cravache* (3 November 1888): 'As far as the things in the *Décadent*, which its director, *specifically* Anatole Baju, claims to hold, and given by whose hands? from Rimbaud, I stand by my denial'—before facing facts, and in light of the manuscript and the envelope postmarked from Aden (see Jules Mouquet, *Rimbaud raconté par Verlaine* [Paris: Mercure de France, 1934], p. 200–1).

France (to Algeria, where he meets up with Germain Nouveau, in early 1894, and to Malta in 1895). André Gide, who met him in Biskra in January 1894, recalled in *If it Die* that he had 'that je ne sais quoi of a vagabond', 'wrapped in white cotton not so much ragged as simple, almost austere' and 'a gaze at once clear and feverish that abruptly saw deep into you, into your soul, only to turn away just as suddenly and get lost far away, in a sort of infinite sadness'. 'From our face-to-face meetings,' Gide added, 'I don't remember either of us speaking very much. But when he would break a long silence and utter a few words, it was his voice—rapid, muted, almost hoarse—that grabbed me.'

The same story is told in Paris, when he meets Claudel, Schwob, Vallette or Léautaud, the primary and rare company he kept. On 31 July 1901, for example, Léautaud notes (recall that after 1891 Rimbaud walked with a slight limp):

> Nine o'clock in the evening. I'm waiting on the Pont-Neuf, in front of the statue of Henri IV, for Schwob: he was the one who had this strange idea. I see a somewhat tall man, limping slightly but with a proud face, neither too thuggish nor not thuggish enough, in a dark-grey suit and, notably, an English cap whose green went very well with his pale complexion. He passes by, with his wooden pipe in his mouth: I recognize Rimbaud, without his beard. 'Well,

how do you like that?!' I say. At first he doesn't respond to my exclamation, no doubt because he doesn't recognize me. Schwob arrives precisely at that moment. 'Rimbaud, don't you recognize Léautaud?' Rimbaud shakes my hand without smiling. We walk a bit towards the rue Dauphine, Schwob excitedly going on and on about his upcoming travel plans, detailing them to Rimbaud in the hopes of benefitting from his patronage. 'It is you—far more than Mallarmé, with his "Flee! Far from here, flee!"—who inspired us to travel.' Rimbaud doesn't respond. I say, 'Not me, thank you. I'm just fine here.' And Schwob continues, citing *African Nights* and even 'The Drunken Boat'. Rimbaud doesn't flinch. Out of pure curiosity, I ask, 'And Gide?' [. . .] All this time Rimbaud hasn't said a word, even looking away which makes him seem like a jerk, while Schwob talks and talks and talks, without noticing anything. We finally part ways at the corner of the rue de Buci, him limping away, his green cap still on his head and his pipe still between his teeth, towards the rue de Seine, and Schwob and I took the rue Saint-André-des-Arts.[13]

The withdrawn, anti-social Rimbaud of 1891–1893 is therefore scarcely distinguishable from what he was

---

13 *Journal littéraire* 1 (31 July 1901).

like a few years before or after. It's to such an extent that, in strictly biographical terms, one could find much more significant interruptions in his later years. For starters, there is 1907, the year of his mother's death and his marriage to Louise Claudel (the rapid succession of these two events has received sufficient commentary).[14] From that point, ensconced in the comfortable quai Voltaire apartment which Louise watches over with enthusiasm and efficiency, the former Charleville runaway, Ogadine explorer, and Harar merchant is finally settled. Admittedly, there are the two great 'relapses' of 1913–1914 (the trip to China) and 1918–1919 (to the United States), but these are less wanderings, marked by the almost metaphysical love of losing oneself, than classic journeys, the second one almost official, as is well known.

From this perspective, the last break that we will attempt to establish in this full and busy life—in 1925—marks a lesser change. Because if, after Louise's death and his marriage, seven months later, to the young Enid Starkie, the ex-adventurer of Africa[15] finally realizes his

14 Vitalie Cuif, aka Widow Rimbaud, dies on 1 August 1907. Arthur marries Louise Claudel, Paul's younger sister and widow of Ferdinand de Massary, on 14 October of the same year. See Suzanne Briet, *Madame Rimbaud: essai de biographie* (Paris: Minard, 1968); Sandro Toni, 'Rimbaud e le donne', *Il Verri* 6 (June 1977); and Alain Borer, 'Mesdames Rimbaud', *Rimbaldiana* 3 (Charleville-Mézières: Musée-Bibliothèque Arthur Rimbaud, 1984).

15 Rimbaud had declared much earlier: 'Finally may there be just one day when I can get out of this slavery and have enough income to

childhood dream ('Ah! Goodness and crikey! Heavens above! I will be independently wealthy'[16]) and completes the circle superbly, the semi-retreat to Charleville would only solidify, far from Paris, the settling down that had begun in Paris in 1907 and was probably decided much earlier. It is true that the conversion to Catholicism, another 'settling down', another phrase applied (apparently) to long wanderings of a spiritual sort, reinforces the importance of 1925 in marking, to use Claude-Edmonde Magny's phrase, 'the last pivotal year' of the Rimbaldian biography.

But in fact, the years 1907 and 1925 are less breaks than confirmations of earlier trends: they would hardly matter without 1891's determined return, which gives them their full meaning. And, above all, they are not punctuated, in his *œuvre*, by loud thunderclaps like the ones in *African Nights*. Except for a few bits of the *System of Modern Life*, which he had been dragging around for eight years; in 1907, Rimbaud wrote practically nothing. *The Black Gospel*, inspired in part by his 1925 conversion, was written afterwards: between 1927–1928. Admittedly, and as we have already noted, we are merely focusing on biography. And yet, creativity or sterility are facts of life. In this sense—and contrary to

---

work only as much as I please!' (Letter to his family, 29 May 1884), or noted philosophically, two years later, 'Man plans on spending three quarters of his life suffering in order to rest during the fourth one' (Letter to his family, Tadjoura, 6 January 1886).

16 'Prologue' (1862).

1891–1893—the years 1907 and 1925 are not particularly exceptional ones, at least not to the point where it is important to refer, in the way that critics refer to a 'first' and a 'second' Rimbaud, to two additional Rimbauds.

For we are not underestimating the importance of the change of 1891–1893 if we consider it to be less radical than that of 1875–1876: for it to seem more attenuated, more progressive, and more predictable, it does not, according to his sister Isabelle's words (which are for once indisputable),[17] make the metamorphosis any less considerable. We certainly go—incrementally, and with fallout, recoils and remorse—from the Rimbaud drunk with solitude to the Rimbaud who will marry twice,[18] from the man who said 'shit to God!' to the

---

17 'The old man [has] completely changed: ideas, opinions, tastes, everything [has] changed.' (Letter to Louis Pierquin, 23 October 1892).

18 Although, as has sometimes been pointed out, his behaviour on this point does not *fundamentally* change: if it is unfair to say, as Étiemble does, that Louise died of the torment and the bad treatment that he dumped on her (Louise *is* no more 'L.' than Rimbaud *is* the narrator of the *Nights*), it sometimes seems that he hardly treats her differently from how he had treated Verlaine thirty years earlier—in fact, he is more often indifferent, 'absent', than aggressive and brutal (see Dominique Férault and Michel Taillefer, 'Rimbaud le solitaire', *Études françaises*, February 1970). As for the permanence (or not) of homosexuality after his adventure with Verlaine and, *a fortiori*, after his first marriage, it is not impossible, even if it is not attested by anything certain. If it is difficult to blindly follow Renaud Camus ('Perseverare rimbaldicum' in *Chroniques achriennes* [Paris: POL,

Catholic, from the vagabond to the sedentary fixture in the place Ducale . . . We won't go so far as the pleasant fiction created by Alain Borer who, in *Rimbaud in Abyssinia*,[19] gives the writer the same fate of his character from *African Nights*, causes him to die around 1891 following an amputation of the leg, and then amuses himself to imagine what we would think about him today, if God had wanted it to be so. (It makes for a small literary game, not without interest and worth practicing on others: How would we view Gide if he had died after *The Fruits of the Earth*; Aragon after the *Treatise on Style* or Joyce after *Dubliners*? . . . ). No. We will agree, however, that this way of rewriting history has the advantage of revealing, in an ingeniously metaphorical way, that one Rimbaud dies in 1891 to give birth to another.[20]

---

1984], pp. 86–98) and all those who have glossed hypothetical links with Crevel or Aragon, neither is there good reason to be as categorical as Paul Claudel who, if only for the obvious family reasons, denied everything wholesale (*Journal littéraire*, 12 November 1925, 4 February 1910, and *passim*), as he already denied the specifics of the relationship with Verlaine, according to Gide's account ('In Dakar [sic] he lived with a local woman [. . .], "which is enough to ruin (says Claudel) the imputations of dubious morals which are sometimes still attached to his name [. . .]." Drawn in for a moment to talk about his relationship with Verlaine, Claudel looks off absently and touches a rosary on the fireplace, in a cup . . . '—*Journal littéraire*, 19 November 1912).

19 Published in 1984 with Éditions du Seuil, in the appropriately named collection 'Fiction & Cie' . . .

20 Needless to say, this criticism-fiction leads Borer to give this truncated Rimbaud a certain coherence, to intimately connect the traveller

Rimbaud in 1921. Photograph by J[ean] Roubier.

. . . and fifty years earlier. Photograph by [Étienne] Carjat.

As such—and this will be our conclusion on this point—if we seek to separate *the* Rimbauds biographically, we must see them not as two but three: the first, too often forgotten, from birth to 1875; the second, from 1875–1876 to 1891; and, lastly, the third, from 1891–1893 until his death. But what about his literary output? Such distinctions no longer hold. Or, rather, we should make one—or even several—per book, lowering ourselves to the crumbling method of textbook authors, blind to the profound unity of a body of work. In truth, from the earliest *Poems* or from *A Season in Hell* to *The Black Gospel* and the unfinished *System of Modern Life*, passing through *African Nights* or *L.*, there was— there *is*— only one Rimbaud. Let us now prove it, with texts as supporting evidence.

## *Anticipating the* Nights

Setting aside the inevitable diversity of genres, pretexts and noticeable themes which—fortunately—are an author's successive works, and thus his separate worlds, a major obstacle presents itself to anyone who looks for

---

of Abyssinia to the adolescent poet, hardening all the traits they have in common—the 'passion for failure' (p. 85), the asocial stance (pp. 115–16), the refusal of sedentary life (pp. 117–18), godlessness (pp. 113–34)—thus pretending to forget that, from the beginning, they are partly counterbalanced by contrary tendencies and that they will largely fade away in the third Rimbaud.

unity: style. Because, if the author in question wrote over a long enough period of time, it is almost inevitable that his style has evolved. Such is the case of Homer between the *Iliad* and the *Odyssey*; of Montaigne from the first to the third book of the *Essays*; of Flaubert from the first *Sentimental Education* to the second one, or from *November* to *Madame Bovary*; of Joyce from *Dubliners* to *Finnegan's Wake*, and of hundreds of others; how could it not be the case for Rimbaud? Especially since for him the changes in *form*—from the first alexandrines to the prose of the *Nights* or to the philosophical proofs of *System of Modern Life*—could only accentuate the differences. In terms of vocabulary alone, Leon Spitzer showed how, from the *Poems* of 1869–1872 to *African Nights*, Rimbaud's palette of words was considerably restrained.[21] It would be all the worse to deny that Rimbaud himself was aware of it, had *wanted* and even explained it, especially in his letter of 13 March 1894 to Huysmans. To the author of *Against the Grain* who apologizes for not mentioning him among Des Esseintes' favourite authors ('You had not published anything yet'), he responds:

It doesn't matter. You were right *in advance*. Des Esseintes probably would have liked the

---

21 'Nebst einem Anhang über die Wortbildung bei Rimbaud in seinen *Nuits d'Afrique*', *Beihefte zur Zeitschrift für romanische Philologie* 32 (1931).

'Decadents', the Bajus, Tailhades and others like them. It's no longer my thing, if it had ever been in the first place: too choppy, too many *turns*, too many words taking themselves too seriously. Now I just try to keep it simple.

We know, in another context, how he will distance himself from Dada:

Too much chaos. I've had my share. Now it is time to build.

And when Roger Gilbert-Lecomte, to whom these words are addressed (2 December 1924), invokes *Illuminations*, he answers:

The *Illuminations* were imposed on me. The opposite of an eccentricity. I could not do them again—especially since such Dadaesque eccentricities can be repeated over and over and over again.[22]

The only one who did not see the difference was Léautaud, who writes the following in 1942, conflating 'The Drunken Boat' with the *Nights*:

*Tuesday 14th April.* Ninth day without bread. Going to Paris after breakfast, next to me, in the subway, a young man reading *African Nights*. A waste of time. He'd do better, as I would have done better at his age, to read other books. 'The

---

22  Letter to Roger Gilbert-Lecomte, 18 December 1924.

green azures,' 'the singing phosphorus,' 'the syringes of the night' [sic]: abracadabratic vocabulary and images.

Léautaud's confusion is interesting. It proves perhaps that original style resists lexical narrowing and syntactical simplifications. In any case, it encourages us to ignore the obstacle we had proposed: after all, according to Valery's formula, style is merely 'the foam of things'. Moreover, he is not the one who will hold us back the most in the few readings that we will attempt: obsessive images (as Charles Mauron or Jean-Paul Weber would say) or the work's major themes will preoccupy us at least as much.

Let us return to Léautaud's amalgam. His mood (or lack of food) is nearly enough to lead the misanthrope of Fontenay to an important truth. In fact, many an image—should we say many a fantasy?—in *African Nights* is already expressed, sometimes down to the word, in poems like 'The Drunken Boat', actually, but also in *A Season in Hell* and some poems in *Illuminations*. Critics of the Lansonian mould, if any remain, will cry out: How could the young man of 1871 or 1873, who has not yet left 'Europe with its ancient parapets', have foreseen what the chronicler of the *Nights* later describes? We will not attempt an answer; instead, let us simply read: for example, one of the first pages of Abel's diary. We are on the lagoon that leads from Suez to the oasis of the Springs of Moses:

We were gliding gently on blue and peaceful waves when, suddenly, the colour of the water changes for no apparent reason: the azure disappears and, as far away as we can see, we discover a choppy, red surface, like waves of blood or rust, with golden reflections shimmering in rays of sunlight. By what instantaneous combination of light effects, married perhaps to billions of animalcules suddenly emerged from the depths under the waves, did this wonder take place? Garelli is as stunned as I am. For the last twenty years that he has been living on the shores of the Red Sea, it is the first time, he tells me, that he has witnessed such a spectacle.

For half or three quarters of an hour, we stay on our path, following this incandescent sea; then, suddenly, the fires go out, the red hue fades, and we find ourselves on the same waves that our oars had just been beating. (I, 5)[23]

Admittedly, this is a travel narrative, as precise as possible, and not the description of a vision. But how does it not make us think of these 'bitter redness of love' 'suddenly dyeing the blueness', to these 'sunfish of the blue wave, the fish of gold' of 'The Drunken Boat', written twenty years earlier? These are verses, of course,

---

23 In references to *African Nights*, Roman numerals refer to chapters, followed by Arabic numerals for page numbers from the first edition published by Mercure de France in 1891.

not the prose 'of Rousseau of the Tropics, of modern Bernardin' that Leon Blum celebrated in his article on the *Nights* that was published in *La Revue blanche* in 1893. Verses, yes, but not unworthy ones. Without too much paradox, one could even prefer their dazzling density, stupefying when they were written, to this more classic and softer prose which sometimes is, as Bernard Frank once said with more than a hint of wickedness, 'at its best, like a better Loti'.

Later, when the expedition finally arrives at Lake Assal after the eventful episode of the attack of the Danakil warriors, the evocation that awaits the reader is not unrelated to the Rimbaud of *Illuminations*:

> In an hour we went down two hundred metres under the sea. At the last thorny grove, leaning my shoulder on a dry trunk, I see an infinite white corolla around a lake. Impossible to express the blindness produced, under the sky far across the sea, by this unbroken, frozen snow.—Sculptures! From the edge of the forest, Buddhas, saints, salt mermaids. On the left, stalactites fall from a cave inhabited by crystal birds. Waves of pale satin flow down, ripple, burst. I advanced on that whiteness, among the eggshells and jewels, on the terraces of marble and ice, and a whiff of brine leaps up and grabs me by the throat. (V, 138)

Same abundance of nominal phrases and, when there is a verb, same dominance of the narrative present; same accumulations of simply juxtaposed words ('Buddhas, saints, salt mermaids', 'flow down, ripple, burst');[24] same topographical precision ('on the left') . . . More troubling than these stylistic analogies, however, is the fact that the Rimbaud of the *Nights* returns to the writing of *Illuminations* precisely in front of a spectacle which, while authentic (everyone who has visited the region and all the present-day travel guides confirm, even with photos, the existence of the band of salt, several kilometres long, with innumerable white forms, that encircles Lake Assal), has so much in common with so many tableaus of *Illuminations*: it is a sunken place, depressed, well below the level of the water (which is, for Lake Assal, at least 170 metres, to be precise), a place that evokes, at random, the following excerpts of the collection of the 1870s:

> The butchers' blocks rose in the dirty main street, and boats were hauled down to the sea, piled high as in pictures. ('After the Flood')

> There is a cathedral coming down and a lake going up ('Childhood' III)

---

24  In *Illuminations*: 'Others support masts, signals, frail parapets' ('Bridges'); ' . . . to the sky that curves, recedes and descends' ('Metropolitan'); ' . . . follow his views, his breaths, his body, his day' ('Genie').

Now hire me for the tomb, whitewashed with the lines of cement in bold relief—far underground. ('Childhood' V)

At a tremendous distance above my subterranean room, houses grow like plants, and fogs gather. The mud is red or black. Monstrous city, endless night! (Ibid.)

They play cards at the bottom of the lake . . . ('Historic Evening')

this last phrase obviously recalling the formula from 'Alchemy of the Word' from *A Season in Hell*:

[. . .] I saw quite frankly [. . .] a parlour at the bottom of a lake [. . .]

To be sure, one could think of Henri Michaux fashioning, on the imaginary themes of the *Voyage in Great Garabagnia* (1936), a prose whose precise simplicity will prove useful twenty years later when he describes his experimentation with drugs in *Miserable Miracle* (1956) and in *Turbulent Infinity* (1957).[25] But there is more here than practice in literary style, and we could say about Rimbaud in Abyssinia what Bernard Frank says about Nerval leaving for the Orient in 1848: 'He is looking for his dreams. He will verify on the ground what he invents in his head'[26] (or rather, for Rimbaud, 'had

---

25 On this topic, we timidly point the reader to our article 'Les Voyages imaginaires de Michaux', *Liberté* 66 (November–December 1969): 7–18.

invented'). To return to the kind of mystery that we mentioned above, everything happens as if *Illuminations* (as well as some passages from *A Season in Hell*, as we will see in a moment) were, in more than one way, premonitions, the dazzling and furtive marks of fantasies that the almost autobiographical adventures of *African Nights* will *realize*. And as if the Rimbaud of the novel—if we can quickly characterize the *Nights* in this way—returns to being, in his writing, the poet of the 1870s each time that this miraculous realization takes place.

The imagery and phrasings are no doubt unique to the *Nights*; for example, the famous metaphor that Breton noted in the first *Manifesto of Surrealism*:

> The thirty-four Abyssinians of our escort sleep under their tents. [. . .] The sharp snigger of hyenas starts up again. I think of Garelli in his hospital room and the blood beneath him. I drink some warm *tej*. I go out, I take a few steps. [. . .] In front of me, emerald grass. Farther afield, a bizarre sketch of mountains, some straight, others curved, still others leaning towards the first ones. In the turquoise sky to the east, blood, stains and syringes of blood of the night. Garelli dies . . . (IV, 99)

---

26 'Digressions', *Le Monde* (14 August 1985), p 11.

This metaphor—which basically associates, in the same proposition, the night in the Danakil Desert and Garelli's agony which the narrator experiences almost as a hallucination—is, incidentally, the exact literary equivalent of superimposition in cinema, of which there is so much in *Summer Party*—Germaine Dulac's 1929 short film based on a screenplay of Rimbaud's (in the close-up, for example, Pierre Batcheff's bloody hands are superimposed on the shot of the girls in their Sunday best along the banks of the Marne).

However, without succumbing to the 'demon of analogy'—like Antoine Adam who tries to connect a phrase from 'Bad Blood' to a minor detail about the travellers' reception when they arrived at King Menelik's court[27]—it is legitimately tempting to note a number of striking proximities between texts separated by twenty years, like the description of the night festival of Mascal, in Adoua, by the narrator suffering from a crushing fever:

> Suddenly the city seems to be in flames. Each inhabitant has lit a fire on his terrace. My servants

27 Arthur Rimbaud, *Œuvres complètes*, VOL. 1 (Paris: Gallimard, 'Bibliothèque de la Pléiade', 1972), p. 1013n26. In the following passage from *African Nights*: ' [. . .] behind him were the warriors, spear in hand and saber at the waist, shoulders adorned with *lebdé*, head uncovered and hair slicked with butter . . . ' (VII, 176), Adam claims finding an echo of the line 'But I don't butter my hair', from *A Season in Hell* . . .

are preparing to do the same on ours [. . .]. On
the market square, under my eyes, heaps of
straw and brush are piled up; with torch in
hand, people come to set them on fire; dances
are organized around these pyres, to the sound
of drums, flutes and clapping hands. Men in war
dress, mounted on their battle horses, engage in
a frenzied carousel, simulating all the twists and
turns of a fight. Gunfire crackles; the children
chase each other with torches; the women
watching these tournaments let out a long,
sharp and mournful cry; people cross the bra-
ziers and launch burning firebrands; long
javelins sparkle, swords strike golden shields,
and *chemmas* appear and disappear as in a phantasmagoria. They are no longer dances, but an
infernal saraband. I'm thirsty, I call Djami and
the others, but no one hears me. The fire gets
bigger, comes right up to me, reaches out,
ignites my brain, my eyes, my limbs . . . (III,
67–8)[28]

Is it so foolish to think of 'Night of Hell' here?
Admittedly, once again the texts are not of the same
genre (intimate, personal assessment here; there, an
adventure story), nor of the same status (allegorical and
visionary here; realistic there). And yet, the comparison

---

28 This description can be compared favourably with the one by
Achille Raffay in *Abyssinie* (Paris: Plon, 1876), p. 106–7.

with Hell is explicit in the *Nights* ('an infernal saraband')
and words, even phrases are repeated from one text to
another ('I'm thirsty', 'The fire gets bigger', in both; 'no
one hears me' in the *Nights*, 'they [the souls] do not hear
me' from the *Season*). The word 'phantasmagoria', also
present in both ('as in a phantasmagoria'—*African
Nights*; 'I am master of phantasmagoria'—*A Season in
Hell*), encourages us, by the way, to formulate a hypothesis: namely, that Rimbaud refers in both cases to images
from magic lanterns as travelling presenters in the eigh-
teenth century showed them to the farthest reaches of
the French countryside and as he probably saw them as
a child.[29] Sabbaths and devilry were among the most
exploited themes. In the rich collection of the
Cinémathèque française (presented to the public for the
first time at the Avignon Festival in August 1985), there
is even a plaque dated 1863 and entitled, precisely,
'Night of Hell' . . .

Finally, one could write an entire doctoral thesis on
the presence—already very strong and insistent, in the
first Rimbaud—of the theme of falling in the mud that
Maurice-Jean Lefebve so insightfully spotted at the end

---

29 Is it necessary, then, to interpret the phrase 'The lantern showed
him [Jesus] to us, standing and pale, with long dark hair, beside an
emerald wave' ('Night in Hell'), where the word 'lantern' appears and
where the abundance of precise colours could lead one to take it for
the description of such an image? It is a hypothesis that we offer to
the regrettably too few specialists of *A Season in Hell* (at present, most
of them are Japanese scholars, like Yoshikazu Nakaji).

of the *Nights* as well as in *The Black Gospel*.[30] For the famous passage in which our hero, whose right leg has just been amputated, falls from his seat in the courtyard of the farm of R***—he drags himself through the mud, drunk with fever, without anybody to pick him up (because his family are at mass), and he is trampled by a horse (XIX, 399–401)—is not without antecedents, without *anticipations*, again, in *A Season in Hell*, in these passages which read like the obsession—and, at the same time, the almost masochistic pleasure—of being 'returned to the ground' ('Farewell'), crushed, shattered and yet not resigned, bursting with a final/ultimate rage:

> I called to my executioners to let me bite the ends of their guns, as I died. I called to all plagues to choke me with sand and blood. Disaster was my god. I stretched out in the mud . . . ('Long ago . . . ')

Much has already been glossed about the 'red, slimy, cold' mud he crawls through, to writhe in pain and burrow his face under the horse's heavy hoof-steps, and its ambiguous value: disgusting and maternal. Following Bachelard, some insisted on its value as a nourishing and demiurgic 'silt' (*Water and Dreams*, p. 148); psychoanalysts, led by Marie Bonaparte, linked mud to excrement (and to the so-coveted gold); Rimbaldians saw 'stench,

---

30 See Maurice-Jean Lefebve, *L'Image fascinante et le surréel* (Paris: Plon, 1965), pp. 286–91.

the ignoble torpor of wine, the belly's shame, nausea',[31] all negative realities that the colour red would connote in Rimbaud's work. Noémi Blumenkranz-Onimus showed[32] the extent to which Marinetti recalled this passage of *African Nights* in the preamble of *Manifesto of Futurism* (1909), when the Italian exalted the 'maternal ditch, half full of muddy water' where he ends up after his car accident:

> I savoured a mouthful of strengthening muck which recalled the black teat of my Sudanese nurse!

However, he noted that this end of the hero of the *Nights* is almost the realistic transposition of the end of 'The Drunken Boat':

> If I desire a water of Europe, it is the black cold puddle . . .

> with its full cohort of negative terms ('I can no longer . . . nor . . . nor . . .') which prefigure the powerlessness, the traveller's final, fatal paralysis?

## *A Disillusioned 'Futurist'*

These similarities (which could be multiplied) will hardly affect those who, like Jacques Bouveresse, take

---

31 Michel Courtois, 'Le Mythe du nègre chez Rimbaud', *Littérature* 11 (October 1973): 91.

32 In 'Marinetti et Rimbaud', *Revue d'esthétique* 5–6 (1978).

Rimbaud, like Musil, for a thinker almost more than for a poet or a novelist.[33] For those colleagues we offer the following observations on Rimbaud as theoretician of 'modern life'.

Critics have often noted the contradiction between the 'Futuristic' texts of 1910–1911—with their exaltation of the city, the speed of the machine, science and 'modernity'—and the bitter, sarcastic and critical pessimism (nearly to the degree of Adorno and the Frankfurt School) that leave their mark in the post-1925 fragments of *System of Modern Life*. We would like to show quickly that there only seems to be a contradiction and that, in any case, its genesis and its key can be found in his early works.

But, first, a word about the label 'Futurist' which was quickly and widely given to the grouping of texts that included the first fragments of *System of Modern Life* (1899–1911), Rimbaud's foreword to the first French translation (by Léon Bazalgette) of Walt Whitman's *Leaves of Grass* (1909) and his letters to Fernando Pessoa (1915–1916). In truth, if Marinetti—who is, as is well known, very quick to add names to his group—does not hesitate, in 1924, in a leaflet *Worldwide Futurism*, to rank Rimbaud (but also Tzara, Breton,

---

33 Jacques Bouveresse, 'Le système de Rimbaud', *Critique* 389 (October 1979): 851–62. At any rate, Bouveresse was right to say that *System of Modern Life*—and not merely because of an identical lack of completion—is Rimbaud's *Man Without Qualities*.

Cocteau and even Drieu La Rochelle and Montherlant!)
among the Futurists:

> *Ecco Arthur Rimbaud, il luminosissimo esploratore*
> *delle sanguinolente notti d'Africa,*[34]

for his part, Rimbaud never expressed, from near or far,
any belonging to the movement. Critics have high-
lighted the kinship of some of his formulas with some
of Marinetti's; for example:

> Sing the streets, the crowds, the tamed rivers,
> the great red factories in the night—O splendid
> cities! (Foreword to *Leaves of Grass*)

Which would be similar to:

> We will sing of the great crowds agitated by
> work, pleasure or revolt; [. . .] the nocturnal
> vibration of arsenals and workshops beneath
> their violent electric moons: gluttonous railway
> stations devouring smoking serpents; factories
> [. . .]; bridges with leaping gymnasts flung
> across the diabolic cutlery of sunny rivers . . .
> (*Manifesto of Futurism*, §11)

However, besides the fact that the two texts are from
the same year and that it is risky to say that Marinetti's,
published in *Le Figaro* on 20 February 1909, is neces-
sarily earlier than Rimbaud's because the printer's
colophon on the translation of *Leaves of Grass* is from

---

34 'Here is Arthur Rimbaud, the dazzling explorer of bloody African
nights.'

June (indeed, the time between the delivery of a manuscript and its appearance in book form is always much longer than between submitting an article and its publication in a newspaper), many of Rimbaud's formulas are evocations, well before Futurism, of verses by Whitman himself, for example from 'Crossing Brooklyn Ferry' (On Brooklyn Lake):

Crowds of men and women [. . .]
[. . .] the fires from the foundry chimneys burning high and glaringly into the night [. . .].
I loved well those cities, loved well the stately and rapid river . . . [35]

But especially—and it is naturally on this point that we want to insist—if they are reminiscent of anyone, it is, first and foremost . . . Rimbaud of the 1870s, who anticipates both the Rimbaud of 1909 and Marinetti (if not Whitman, too: his quoted verses date from 1856, but Rimbaud would only discover them—as he explains in the foreword—in 1900):

The terrible mob with the sounds of the ocean swell . . . ('The Blacksmith')

. . . We are
For the great new times when men will want to know,

---

35 Walt Whitman, *Leaves of Grass / Feuilles d'herbe* (Roger Asselineau trans.) (Paris: Aubier-Flammarion, 'bilingue', 1972).

When Man will forge from morning to night
. . . (Ibid.)

In cities [. . .] I saw a sea of flames and smoke in
the sky . . . (*A Season in Hell*, 'Bad Blood')

And, at dawn, armed with an ardent patience, we
will enter magnificent cities. (Ibid., 'Farewell')

The truth is that Rimbaud does not get caught up
in it, not more than Apollinaire, who will be much more
compromised for all the time he spends with Marinetti.
The irony that sometimes appears in Apollinaire's *The
Futurist Anti-Tradition* (for example, how he dated it:
'Paris, 29 June 1913 [. . .] from 65 metres above the Boul.
S.-Germain', no doubt to make fun of how Marinetti
dated and situated each text from up in an aeroplane . . . )
can be felt, and oh how much more explicitly, in a letter
to Pessoa on 16 June 1915:

Your friend Sá-Carneiro handed me *Orpheu*.
Somehow I read it despite my still bumbling
Portuguese. [. . .] Am struck by the 'marinet-
tism' of it all. Strange that these fumes are still
swirling around in your head. Yesterday, Sá-
Carneiro grabbed me for an hour with a tract
of italic [*sic*] paints (Balla, etc.). And he didn't
even bother to look at a Picasso; Picasso is
much stronger—the only one, with Kandinski
(do you know him?). [. . .] No, I assure you: a
little less *Zang Tumb Tumb* and a little more

thought! Cars will not save the world. Nor will electricity. *Por amor de Deus, tirem-me daqui a metafísica*! *Se têm a verdade, guardem-na*! As your friend De Campos says: *Fora*! *Fora*![36]

> Your A. R.

In fact—and to return to our main point—the geometric place of Rimbaud's thoughts on the modern world is closer to pessimism for the end of days than the joyous tirades à la Verhaeren or Whitman—for whom there is always a degree of an impalpable irony:

> Long live jet locomotives with beautiful steaming rumps—although I prefer my horse and my legs . . . (Foreword to *Leaves of Grass*)

The seemingly euphoric developments of the *System* on the liberating city (Fragments 10, 12, 24–28, 113, etc.), on the speed of communication (Fragments 7 and 8), and on the emancipation of the working class (where there are several well-known allusions to Marx and Bakunin) belong to a limited and very well-circumscribed period, of the book's genesis, and it is more than probable that, if Rimbaud had been able to finish it, he would have altered them or even removed them entirely. Certainly, at the time of the Popular Front and the triumph of his old acquaintance Leon Blum, he seems reluctant to deny or even amend what he wrote thirty years earlier,

---

36 'For the love of God, take me away from all the metaphysics! If they have the truth, let them keep it! [. . .] Scram! Scram!'

particularly on socialism and the emancipation of the colonies, but his last letter to Thomas Mann leaves little doubt about his real intentions:

> Received your lecture on Freud. Appreciated that you have illuminated (with Enlightenment!) comrade Nietzsche's phrase: '*Reaktion als Fortschritt.*'[37] Would you believe that I now think the converse is true: progress as a form of reaction. Settembrinis[38] are admirable, but are they anything but improved versions of Messieurs Homais & Prudhomme? *Heute abend wird getanzt*!, etc., etc.[39] In spite of what is going on in France at the moment, I do not see that the West, your dear West, is choosing the path of pleasant dreams. If I ever finish (*endlich*! . . . ) my *System*, we shall see. [. . .] The Hoptimist [*sic*] that I still was, slightly, when we first met, is now dead and buried. It remains for me to draw the consequences in the book's very organization (if the Devil or Hitler does not take me first) . . . (10 December 1936)

---

37 'Reaction as a form of progress', allusion to the title of one of the sections of *Human, Too Human* commented by Thomas Mann in 'Freud in the History of Modern Thought', a speech delivered in Munich in 1929 and sent to Rimbaud in German in 1936.

38 Allusion to a character from *The Magic Mountain*, prototype of the radical-socialist humanist.

39 'There will be dancing tonight!'

Rimbaud in his garden, Charleville, 1931.

The same thoughts are on display in an interview with André Rousseaux in 1935. When asked a question about Giono, Rimbaud responds:

> *Regain* touches me. The land, the wheat: very little for me, but I understand deep down inside myself. I am bound by the palms of my hands, by the soles of my feet. Contrary to what you might think. Alas, the very idea of regain or renewal is ephemeral. I see that this world cuts itself off from the earth, to head to the cities. It's a matter of just two or three generations. We will mechanize everything. I don't know what we'll eat. The land, the wheat, Giono, all these beautiful French *pastoral tales*: soon it will all be mythology and the like. (*Le Figaro*, 28 September 1935)

In other words, even if he sometimes proclaims it against himself, and perhaps all the more strongly because his first inclination for optimism was already strong to begin with, his true vision of the 'world the day after tomorrow' can be found in formulas like:

> *Reason.* Reasonable devils shall come. Their reason will be at the tips of their fork. (Fragment 613, 1929?)

> Reason and science swallowed as a poison by the enemies of *the free man*. Mithridates. Good turned into evil, and against us. (Fragment 810, 1935)

*Cities.* As *entourage*, families, clans, classes, even nations will pass. There will come a day when we will live only for ourselves. I do not like myself any more: I kill myself. Dust of solitude waiting for the lethiferous potion. (Fragment 501, 1925)

*Giants.* The Russian giant, the American giant, the German giant (or others). One will swallow all the others. We will all be swallowed. Merchants, rulers and 'intellectuals' will be scrambling—the French elite! They will be the first to be gobbled up. Amid the chaos, they will sell off everything: Joan of Arc and Racine, customs and speech patterns. March to the Spirit! Uniformity. First-century Rome. But what about the barbarians who will avenge us, where will they come from? No more barbarians, eternal rest. (Fragment 782, 1934)

What is particularly notable here is that this double contradictory movement—in which the second (ironic, critical) outweighs the first (ardent, enthusiastic)—is already present, if we read attentively, in the Rimbaud of the 1870s. The progressive, pre-'Futurist', almost positivist, proclamations cited above are counterbalanced by formulas of the opposite tone:

I was able to expel from my mind all human hope. (*A Season in Hell*, 'Long ago . . . ')

> I am not prisoner of my reason. (*A Season in Hell*, 'Bad Blood')

—or, simply, struck by irony (as one would say, 'struck by helplessness'). Who could argue that there is enthusiasm or even simple buy-in in passages such as:

> The inferior race has covered everything: the people, as they say; reason, nation and science. Oh! Science! Everything has been reconsidered. For the body and the soul—the viaticum—there is medicine and philosophy—old wives' remedies and rearranged popular songs. [. . .]
>
> Science, the new nobility! Progress. The world marches on! Why shouldn't it turn back? (Ibid.)

At most, it is an *analysis* (the contemporary and convergent development of rationalism, science and the idea of nation is linked to the emancipation of the third state—the 'people', as they say). Nothing suggests that Rimbaud is pleased about it, or that he does anything more than observe. One could note the flippant tone, the hint of sarcasm—along with an ahistorical vision of things—in such *genealogies* of medicine and philosophy.

'Mr Prudhomme was born with Christ'; 'the modern Ecclesiastes, namely, *Everyone*': the Rimbaldian vision of the heroes of the modern world is anything but complacent. Science? It 'doesn't move fast enough' ('The Impossible'). This is one more constraint, tied to loathed work (the beginning of 'Lightning'). Thank goodness!

. . . People will get along without me.
('Lightning')

In short, the key to the ambiguities of *System of Modern Life* is in *A Season in Hell*: it is less a question of fixed, lasting contradictions than of a sometimes violent back-and-forth between a first position and a second one, the latter prevailing in the long run and erasing, so to speak, the former, but without erasing it completely, like a palimpsest on which earlier text is still visible. This is what Thomas Mann had foreseen in his 'Über Rimbaud' of 1934, shortly after the publication of *Looking Without Eyes*. Making a great deal of Thierry Maulnier's criticisms ('Mr Rimbaud obviously thinks that we are blind. Between what he wrote twenty years ago and today, there is no evolution, just incoherence'), Mann speaks of two complementary Rimbauds:

. . . *diese Verschränktheit ist eine immer wiederkehrende Erscheinung*[40]

In truth, it would be necessary to speak of a dialectic, but of a dialectic that does not succeed. Such is the meaning of Barthes's well-known analysis:

We know that the dialectic, from Plato to Hegel (or Marx), changes in number: from two to three. The oratorical alternation of the dialogue gives way to a duel's third *resolution* (thesis and

---

40 'each one is intertwined in the other by a constantly renewed phenomenon', 'Über Rimbaud', a speech delivered at the University of Vienna, 17 April 1934.

antithesis transmuted in synthesis). [. . .] For Rimbaud, it's not two or three, but two and a half. The second term prevails over the first, but the resolution does not seal one's victory over the other. It partially preserves the thesis under the antithesis. It is a semi-victory, a suspended erasure: a *deletus* (Tertullian), but a *deletus interruptus*.[41]

In sum, Rimbaud's true place is the burning root of contradiction, the unsustainable moment when we go from yes to no, from white to black. While thinkers usually surpass and forget this moment, Rimbaud returns to it, obstinately, and *revels* in it, as if by consensual curse. 'This spirit is located, and in a frightening way, at the centre of all our anxieties,' said Benjamin Fondane in 1933. It should be added: and of his anxieties, too. It is from this point that we can raise the issue of masochism with respect to *The Black Gospel*—although we proposed this term earlier, to characterize some aspects of *A Season in Hell*.

In this sense, Rimbaud's 'contradictions' are not aesthetic—in the sense of the Kierkegaardian 'aesthetic stage'—contrary to what many critics (including Étiemble) wrote in the 1940s (and even though attempting to bring *L.* closer to *The Seducer's Diary*). We can

---

41 'La dialectique avortée de Rimbaud', *Rimbaud/Artaud/Michaux*, special issue of *Revue esthétique* (1979).

hardly confuse them either with an ethics of 'alternating' à la Montherlant or with the refusal to choose as in Gide's *Nourritures terrestres*. Gide himself said it so well:

> Any paths that opened to me, waiting, I didn't waste any time hemming and hawing over which one to follow, even if, once I had taken it, I would have preferred the other one. Such was the case with my play *Saül*, which I wrote immediately after *Nourritures* as a kind of antidote [. . .]. But Rimbaud proceeds differently: he moves forward while keeping his head half turned in the direction that he's abandoning, not so much with regret as with the secret certainty of having to return—and all the more painfully. He sometimes does this in a hurry, as in this passage from *L.* (the Night in Brussels) in which I feel that I can already hear the sobs of *The Black Gospel*.[42]

### Insomniac Forever

Our last demonstration is inspired by Gide. For if, indeed, the particularly violent scene of the 'slaps on the Grand-Place' (the narrator, claiming to be in a fury, even hit *L.* right in the centre of Brussels, in the middle of a crowd of baffled strollers) is followed by a sort of half-sarcastic, half-anguished change of heart which is,

---

42 *Journal littéraire*, 29 September 1929.

as Mauriac said, 'one of the few human moments in this satanic book':

> What have I done? God would disapprove of
> me. Dear God. But this wicked joy that so ani-
> mated my tongue and my hand, isn't it a divine
> joy? Wasn't it once the joy of the Great
> Impatient One, the Great Punisher of the Old
> Testament? By hitting him, it is myself that I
> hit, that much is sure.[43]

Conversely, the middle of Book 2 of *The Black Gospel* amazes us with its sudden return to a wild and boundless hedonism, a sort of 'relapse' that made Ramon Fernandez say that we were 'suddenly in the *Nourritures terrestres* as revised by Sade and Masoch'[44] and in which Claudel saw 'the passage of the Cunning One':

> My dear body! I am Orpheus and the hetaerae.
> Each extremity stretched out to capture infinite
> pleasure, palm and skin, up to committing
> crimes, and offering itself to be devoured.
> Hosanna![45]

But these sudden reversals, these violent reservations—these 'fickle comings and goings between Sade and John of the Cross' (Claude-Edmonde Magny),

---

43 Arthur Rimbaud, *L.* (Paris: Gallimard, 'Folio'), p. 112.

44 'La conversion de Rimbaud', *Nouvelle revue française* (January 1929).

45 Arthur Rimbaud, *L'Évangile noir* (Paris: Gallimard, 'Folio', 1928), p. 54.

one could say between the two Baudelairian 'postula-tions'—are already in *A Season in Hell*, a very important text, with their incessant about-turns, strong as rages and angry outbursts that gradually fade to the point of *relative* appeasement. Let us recall, for the record, some of the seismograph's movements:

. . . I have always belonged
to an inferior race.
[. . .] I am dancing the sabbath
in a red clearing . . . ('Bad Blood' II)

We are moving towards the *Spirit*.
('Bad Blood' II)

The pagan blood returns!
('Bad Blood' III)

Gluttonously I am waiting for God. [. . .]
. . . I am leaving Europe.
[. . .] Saved. ('Bad Blood' III)

Now I am an outcast . . .
('Bad Blood' III )

You cannot get away.
('Bad Blood' IV)

. . . oh my marvellous charity!
('Bad Blood' IV)

. . I have never been Christian.
.] I am a beast, a savage. ('Bad Blood' V)

Simply, what in 1873 is condensed in the few pages of a single text is then developed, *orchestrated*, from one major text to another. With, certainly, longer lulls, especially after the conversion, the relative triumph of 'grace' over 'pagan blood', although—still the 'aborted dialectic'!—without getting any closer to a truly definitive *resolution*. All the testimonies that we have about the last days of the 'patriarch of Charleville', according to Pierre de Boisdeffre's so ill-fitting phrase, paint the same picture of an irreparably tormented man. For example, this is how he was seen by the young André Pieyre de Mandiargues, who made the pilgrimage to Charleville in December 1936:

> Although it was late and everyone was now asleep in the house on the Place Ducale, one of the quietest and most austere houses that I was given to visit, Rimbaud was not even remotely tired. He went silently from one wall of the library to the other with abrupt movements and unpredictable stops that, because of his white beard and the linen garment that he wore, made him look like a snow statue or an owl fluttering around in the chalky dust of a lime kiln.[46]

---

46 One will be struck to find a similar image, again about himself, in a letter that Rimbaud wrote to his family dated 1878. Crossing the Gotthard through the snow—'the white nuisance'—the traveller notes: 'Without the shadow one is oneself, and without the telegraph poles, which follow the supposed road, one would be as embarrassed

'Insomniac': I do not know of a word more down-to-earth, almost medical, and which is also certainly out of place in describing a writer who is among the most divine, one could say, that this country has ever seen. And yet, it is the word that somehow seemed obvious in defining the skinny old man who now stared at me with his crystal-clear eyes where it seemed that all the sadness of the world was concentrated. Insomniac—insomniac, anyone would have chosen the word, always and forever.[47]

This is well known and it is amply confirmed by the portraits from the end of his life: the ones by Matisse or Marie Laurencin as well as the photo that Cartier-Bresson took during Rimbaud's last public appearance, between Gide and Malraux at the 1935 Writers' Congress.

We will not have wasted our time if, at the end of this too-brief study, it was accepted that this 'insomnia forever' can already be sensed in Carjat's photographic portraits of young Rimbaud (especially the one from December 1871), in the same way that the great works of 1893, 1910 or 1928 contain—and how brilliantly—the seeds of his early works. In this sense, we disagree

as Pierrot in an oven.' Is this, then, the image of Rimbaud that we should keep, from start to finish: A man lost in whiteness?

47 André Pieyre de Mandiargues, 'Le Poète insomniaque' (1937). Reprinted in *Deuxième Belvédère* (Paris: Grasset, 1962).

with Pierre-Henri Simon's hasty remark from 1966 ('research on Rimbaud has little to teach us'): in the comparative path that we have taken here, Rimbaud studies have a bright future ahead of them.

# NOTES TO THE ENGLISH EDITION

*The Three Rimbauds* | For the title, Noguez borrows an idea proposed by Paul Claudel in his foreword to the 1912 edition of Rimbaud's *Complete Works*, in which Claudel claimed that the three periods in Rimbaud's literary life were characterized by violence, the seer period and mastery:

> As short as Rimbaud's literary life was, it is possible to identify three periods, three modes. The first is of violence, of the pure male, of the blind genius emerging as a burst of blood, like an unrestrainable cry, in verses of an unheard-of force and stiffness [. . .] The second period is that of the seer. In a letter of 15 May 1871 [. . .] Rimbaud tried to make us understand the 'method' of this new art which he inaugurates—and which is really an alchemy, a kind of transmutation, a spiritual decantation of the elements of this world. In this need to 'escape' which only lets go of him at his death, in this desire to 'see' which even as a child made him crush his eyes with his fist (see 'The Seven Year Old Poets'), there is much more than vague romantic nostalgia. [. . .] It is here that

> Rimbaud, having arrived at the full mastery of his art, makes us hear this marvellous prose, its intelligible sound permeating to its smallest fibres, like the soft, dry wood of a Stradivarius.

—Paul Claudel, *Nouvelle revue française* 8 (1912): 559–63.

PAGE 17 | *Paul Valéry . . . welcomed the new academician*: No such speech exists, although Valéry delivered one the following year (22 January 1931), when Marshal Philippe Pétain succeeded Marshal Ferdinand Foch on Seat 18 (Pétain would be forced to give up his 'immortality' after the Second World War). In his address—the only one that Valéry delivered during the election of a fellow academician—Valéry praised Pétain for never forgetting that 'the real is nothing more than an unorganized and infinite number of particular cases, which must be considered carefully each time and then re-evaluated'. As Bernard Frank explained ('Littérature en liberté', *Le Monde*, 17 April 1986):

> Noguez started from the simple idea that I mentioned in an old 'Digression' column that, as they are just two years apart, Pétain and Rimbaud are of the same generation. While he buried Rimbaud in 1937, Noguez is less generous in nature with the Marshal, who died in 1951: Rimbaud still had time to be welcomed into the Académie française by Paul Valéry in

1930, a year after Pétain. His fictional life was
therefore not completely hopeless.

*man with the soles of wind*: Paul Verlaine's now-famous
expression '*l'homme aux semelles de vent*' that he used to
describe his peripatetic friend first appeared in two letters from Ernest Delahaye to Verlaine towards the end
of the summer of 1878: '[T]he man with the soles of wind
has been wiped off the map. Not a trace.'—Arthur
Rimbaud, *Correspondance* (Jean-Jacques Lefrère ed.)
(Paris: Fayard, 2007), p. 243. Then in another letter on
31 December 1881: 'Following your information about
the hypothetically Roche-dwelling "Monster", I wrote
to him in at his mother's house. Mme Rimbe tells me that
"poor Arthur" is presently in Arabia, Harat or Harar: I
can't make out what she wrote. I will write to Mme
Rimbe today to ask her to forward my little love note if
she knows the exact address of "the Man with the soles
of wind".'—Rimbaud, *Correspondance*, p. 297. The quotation marks suggest that Verlaine had coined the phrase,
as Delahaye would suggest in an article in 1906: 'The
adventures of "the man with the soles of wind", as he
called him, were celebrated in silly *dizains* [ten-line
poems] that he called "Coppées".'—Ernest Delahaye,
'Le séjour de Paul Verlaine dans les Ardennes (1877–
1883)', *Revue d'Ardennes et d'Argonne* 4–5 (February–
March 1906): 61.

*a brief 'Night of Hell'* . . . *himself a 'drunken boat'*:
References to two poems by Rimbaud, 'Night in Hell'

from *A Season in Hell* and the verse poem 'The Drunken Boat'.

PAGE 18 | FOOTNOTE 1: The Breton quotation originally comes from Rimbaud's poem 'Delirium I. The Foolish Virgin' from *A Season in Hell*.

*in the journal* Les Trois Roses, *published in Grenoble*: See André Breton's prose poem 'Âge', *Les Trois Roses* 2 (July 1918): 29; Louis Aragon, 'Pur Jeudi', *Les Trois Roses* 3–4 (August–September 1918): 46. For more on *Les Trois Roses*, see Laurence Campa, *Poètes de la grande Guerre* (Paris: Éditions Classiques Garnier, 2010), p. 22.

Quotation from Aragon, including verses from 'Doctrine': The Rimbaud forgeries 'Doctrine' and 'Omega' appeared in the pages of *Le Décadent* in 1888. In all, six fake Rimbaud poems were published in *Le Décadent*: 'Sonnet' (29 November 1886); 'Instrumentation' (1–15 January 1888); 'The Horned Females' (1–15 February 1888); 'The Snail' (15–31 May 1888); 'Doctrine' (1–15 July 1888) and 'Blasphemous Omega' (15–30 September 1888). Noguez indeed quotes a passage from *Le Libertinage*, and substitutes his imagined Rimbaud into it:

> 'The Parameters', 'The Ice Cabinet' or 'At the Base of the Wall' are similarly the fruits of *Alcide*'s dandyism and 'The Principled Damsel': between them it is possible to trace the path taken. With 'The Ice Cabinet', Lenore has

stopped in the scene that is being played out, between the young man and her, to be this model that is a composite of the Céline from 'The Damsel' and the 'Well-Bred Young Girl' from *Alcide*.

—Louis Aragon, *Œuvres romanesques complètes*, VOL. 1 (Daniel Bougnoux and Philippe Forest eds) (Paris: Gallimard, 'Bibliothèque de la Pléiade', 1997), pp. 265–6.

As for the verses, they are forgeries of forgeries: they are Noguez's creations, rather than quotations from *Le Décadent*.

PAGE 19 | Examples quoted by Breton: The first paragraph comes from Rimbaud's poem 'Cities' (of the two poems with that title, the one that begins 'They are cities!').— Arthur Rimbaud, *Complete Works, Selected Letters* (Wallace Fowlie trans, Seth Whidden revised ed) (Chicago: University of Chicago Press, 2005), p. 328. Subsequent references to Rimbaud's work refer to this translation. Unattributed translations are my own.

*the break-up between the author of* African Nights *and the Surrealist movement*: By the time *Second Manifesto of Surrealism* appeared in 1929, Breton was already distancing himself from certain interpretations of Rimbaud— 'It's useless to discuss Rimbaud again: Rimbaud was wrong, Rimbaud wanted to fool us. He is guilty in our eyes for having allowed, for not having made completely impossible, certain disparaging interpretations of his thoughts (such as those made by Paul Claudel).'

PAGE 20 | FOOTNOTE 2: The original letter-tract is accurately cited.

FOOTNOTE 3: Noguez situates this imaginary essay at the time of the scandal of the Closerie des Lilas, where the publication *Les Nouvelles littéraires* had convened a dinner on 2 July, presided over by Rachilde, to honour poet Saint-Pol Roux. A heated debate erupted over various political differences, with additional fuel provided by the famous open letter to Claudel written that same week. See Béatrice Mousli, *Philippe Soupault* (Paris: Flammarion, 2010), pp. 168–70.

*mouth of light*: This phrase sits in contrast with '*la bouche d'ombre*' (the mouth of darkness), which Rimbaud lifted from a poem in Victor Hugo's collection *Les Contemplations* and used to refer to his mother.

'*I have never been Christian*' and '*That would be the French way of life, the path of honour*': Both quotations from this paragraph are from 'Bad Blood' in *A Season in Hell* (*Complete Works*, p. 275 and 271, respectively).

PAGE 21 | FOOTNOTE 4: The first Nobel Prize for literature was awarded in 1901 to Sully Prudhomme, whose poem Rimbaud had once plagiarized on his way to winning a school prize; see Seth Whidden, *Arthur Rimbaud* (London: Reaktion, 'Critical Lives,' 2018), p. 18. Since he had died in 1891, Rimbaud was not considered for the 1937 award, which went to fellow Frenchman Roger Martin du Gard (1881–1958).

Quotation from *Anthology of Black Humour*: This passage is a combination of Breton's original and Noguez's additions. In the original, Breton wrote that:

> For one thing, [Rimbaud's] inner and outer selves never managed to coexist harmoniously. They alternate, and even interfere with each other constantly, in his early years. We will ignore his later years—when the puppet took over, when a pathetic clown waved his money belt around every other minute—and consider only the Rimbaud of 1871–1872, a veritable god of puberty, the likes of which no mythologies had ever seen.

—André Breton, *Anthologie de l'humour noir* (Paris: Jean-Jacques Pauvert, 1966), p. 280.

While Rimbaud did carry around a money belt, he hardly waved it around proudly, as he explained to his family: 'I am desperately tired at present, and at present I have no job. I fear losing the little I have. Just think: I always carry, in my belt, sixteen thousand and a few hundred francs in gold; it weighs about eight kilos and gives me dysentery'—Letter to his family, 23 August 1887 (*Complete Works*, p. 435).

*We are living in Galeries Lafayette Ducasse-Rimbaud*: The quotation comes from Paul Éluard, mocking Cocteau, in response to questions from the Belgian surrealist journal *Le Disque vert* for a special issue about Lautréamont (in VOL. 2, 1925, p. 95). After putting words in the mouth of Jean Hytier, Jean Cassou, Joseph Delteil, Marce'

Arland, Albert Thibaudet, Maurice Maeterlinck and Paul
Valéry, Éluard wrote:

> And then, without blushing, because we will
> end up slaughtering him like a 'stinking' beast,
> let's talk about Jean Cocteau. Prudence has
> never stopped anyone from being foul. '*We live
> in Galeries Lafayette, Ducasse Rimbaud, etc. The
> House of Isidore-Arthur and Company, Max,
> Radiguet and I were the only ones to get a whiff
> of the thing. This is the basis of our misunder-
> standing with the youth.*' '*Got a whiff of the
> thing,*' such carrion was actually at the Steam
> Baths, not at the Galeries Lafayette.

—Paul Éluard, 'Le Cas Lautréamont, d'après le "Disque
Vert"', *La Révolution surréaliste* 6 (1 March 1926): 3.
Reprinted in *Œuvres complètes*, VOL. 2 (Marcelle Dumas
and Lucien Scheler eds) (Paris: Gallimard, 'Bibliothèque
de la Pléiade,' 1968), pp. 804–5. See also Gabriel Götz,
'1925—Montevideo in the Orient: Lautréamont's Ascent
Among the Paris Surrealists', *Journal of Surrealism and
the Americas* 3(1–2) (2009): 51–83.

PAGE 22 | FOOTNOTE 5: No such article exists; instead, here
Noguez modifies Cocteau's foreword to *J'adore* by Jean
Debordes, published in 1928. Cocteau had originally
written:

> Young people who listen to me, who look at me,
> who believe me, young people from all over,

from the old world and the new world, I climb up to a balcony high in the air that looks out over the walls they are trying to put between us, the lies and my legend, and I say to you: this book teaches the new anarchy which consists in loving God without limits, in letting go of caution and in saying all that you feel in your heart.

—Jean Cocteau, Foreword to Jean Desbordes, *J'adore* (Paris: Grasset, 1928), p. 12.

While there is no mention of Cocteau or Desbordes in *Le Figaro* on 17 February 1928, the newspaper began its 21 September issue with Camille Mauclair's review of *J'adore*. Its criticism of the celebrity attributed to authors is not without echoes of the Rimbaud myth, which Desbordes seems to follow at several key moments: his early writings dazzled Cocteau as Rimbaud's had done to Verlaine, and in each case the elder's public support (the essay in *Les Poètes maudits*, the foreword to *J'adore*) brought instant name recognition to a relative unknown. In 1928, Mauclair referred to the unheard-of tone with which Cocteau glorified this previously unknown poet:

I have never seen Mr Jean Desbordes and I know nothing about him other than that some are trying to put him in a position to profit from this machine of fame which these days quickly produces a sort of lifetime celebrity, payable in instalments. [. . .] I know full well that a sad recent practice thinks it clever to begin not with the premises of solid and scrupulous talent, but with some scandal: obscene, absurd, immoral, or spitting on the fatherland, just pick one, to create a lot of buzz and spread the name. Once a following is created, many return to the usual formulas like good little bourgeois, delighted to have hastened a launch that merit alone would have made one wait longer. It is a literary strategy, despicable to be sure, but it must be taken into account.

—Camille Mauclair, 'Pour l'honneur des Lettres', *Le Figaro*, 21 September 1928, p. 1.

PAGE 23 | *lansonism*: An approach to literary study championed by Gustave Lanson (1857–1934): beginning with rigorous philological approach and a heavy reliance on inductive reasoning from source materials, it was generalized to represent the dogma of positivist criticism popular in universities prior to post-structuralism.

PAGE 24 | Year 1891: It is the year of Rimbaud's death—he died on 10 November at the Hôpital de la Conception in Marseilles—rather than his secret return to Paris. See Whidden, *Rimbaud*, p. 176.

On Antoine Adam dating 'Devotion' and 'Democracy', from *Illuminations*, to 1876: In 'L'énigme des *Illuminations*', *Revue des sciences humaines*, fascicule 60

(October–December 1950): 221–45, Adam situates 'Democracy' after Rimbaud's time in the Dutch navy (pp. 223–5), and 'Devotion' after his stay in Milan (p. 231).

PAGE 25 | FOOTNOTE 6: Richard does indeed devote a chapter of his study to what he calls 'La Mystification des faux Rimbaud' (The Mystification of fake Rimbauds), pp. 201–13.

FOOTNOTE 7: Armand Savouré sent his letter, dated 3 April 1930, to Georges Maurevert, editor of *L'Éclaireur de Nice*. A facsimile was reproduced in Alain Borer, *Un Sieur Rimbaud se disant négociant* (Paris: Lachenal et Ritter, 1984), p. 76.

*travel notes plundered by Henri Donbiville*: A fictitious reference.

PAGE 28 | *in a rue Visconti mansard*: The small street where Balzac set up his printing press, and lived above what would be a commercial failure, between 1826 and 1828, rue Visconti is also where Jean Racine died in 1699, and Eugène Delacroix lived and worked from 1835 to 1844.

FOOTNOTE 8: Gustave Kahn told Jules Huret that Rimbaud was a great forgotten poet whom Lautrémont could not fully replace.

*15 rue de l'Échaudé-Saint-Germain*: This was the address when Alfred Vallette took over the reins of Mercure de France in 1890; he lived above the shop, and Rachilde joined him there when they were married in June 1889. See Melanie Hawthorne, *Rachilde and French Women's Authorship*: *From Decadence to Modernism* (Lincoln: University of Nebraska Press, 2001), pp. 135–6. Mercure de France moved to its present address in rue de Condé in 1908.

PAGE 29 | FOOTNOTE 9: No letters from Rimbaud are dated 1892, that is, after his death in 1891.

FOOTNOTE 10: A plaque at No. 4 rue de Vaugirard attests to Verlaine's presence there, intermittently, between March 1889 and December 1894.

PAGE 30 | *I was working for the glove-maker Berr* . . . : Noguez draws on Léautaud's own diary in which he describes working as a *tribun*:

> When I was 'gallery assistant' working for the glove-maker Berr, my predecessor had left the sum of 16 francs and a few centimes in the desk, a counting error, I think. I would take the money out, I'd put it back, I'd take it back out again. One day I didn't put it back. (9 January 1924)

—Paul Léautaud, *Journal littéraire* 4 (1922–24): 254.

PAGE 31 | FOOTNOTE 11: While this meeting between child-hood friends Léautaud (1872–1956) and Van Bever (1871–1927) is imagined—there is no mention of Van Bever or Rimbaud in Léautaud's diary entry from 26 January 1937—they did collaborate on the biographical sketch of Rimbaud in *Poètes d'aujourd'hui, morceaux choisis accompagnés de notices biographiques et d'un essai de bibliographie*, VOL. 2 (Paris: Mercure de France, 1900), pp. 154–63.

FOOTNOTE 12: The account of Verlaine's alleged retraction is fictitious.

*invited to participate in the Académie . . . he refuses almost indignantly*: While Edmond de Goncourt began plan-ning the Académie Goncourt upon his brother Jules's death in 1870, and included it in the will that he dictated in 1892, the idea was held up in the courts from Edmond's own death in 1896—pitting literary executors Alphonse Daudet and Léon Hennique, represented by future French president Raymond Poincaré, against family members—until it was finally resolved in March 1900. See Léon Deffoux, *Du Testament à l'académie Goncourt, suivi d'une petite chronologie du Testament de l'Académie et du prix Goncourt* (Paris: Société anonyme d'éditions et de librairie, 1920).

PAGE 32 | *that je ne sais quoi of a vagabond*: Biskra is the setting in André Gide's *The Fruits of the Earth* (1897) and *The Immoralist* (1902). He spent a fortnight in the town in February 1895 with Lord Alfred Douglas, following a meeting with Oscar Wilde in Blida and Algiers.

PAGE 33 | *Flee! Far from here, flee!—who inspired us to travel*: the line is from Stéphane Mallarmé's poem 'Sea Breeze': 'The flesh is sad, alas! And I've read all the books. / Flee! Far from here, flee!! / I feel that the birds are drunk.

FOOTNOTE 13: A fictitious journal entry.

PAGE 34 | FOOTNOTE 14: While Suzanne Briet's *Madame Rimbaud* was indeed published in 1968, the reference to Sandro Toni article is fictional. As is the Alain Borer article; in that issue of *Rimbaldiana* he contributed an article entitled 'Rimbaud dans le "Grand Jeu"' (pp. 5–10), in which he discusses Rimbaud's work but does not mention his mother.

Enid Starkie: In *Rimbaud in Abyssinia* (1937), Enid Starkie's claims made Rimbaud's possible involvement in slave trade seem plausible, at least for twenty-five years until they were finally debunked by Mario Matucci in *Le Dernier Visage de Rimbaud en Afrique* (1962).

FOOTNOTE 15: The letters are accurately cited.

PAGE 35 | FOOTNOTE 16: This passage is quoted from Rimbaud's early prose work (*c.* 1864–65), 'The sun was still hot [. . .]' (*Complete Works*, p. 221).

*the last pivotal year*: See Claude-Edmonde Magny, 'Arthur Rimbaud', *Poètes d'aujourd'hui* 12 (1954). While this phrase is not in Magny's article, she rejects the notion of there being two Rimbauds: 'Rimbaud the Thug is inseparable from Rimbaud the Seer.'

PAGE 36 | FOOTNOTE 17: As the parentheses indicate, Noguez alters the verb tense, which Isabelle had originally written in the pluperfect; otherwise the passage is quoted verbatim.

FOOTNOTE 18: The Férault–Taillefer article is fictitious, as are the references to the chapter in Camus's *Chroniques achriennes* and any mention of Rimbaud in Claudel's journals on those dates. Gide's account, which does indeed detail a meeting with Rimbaud's posthumous brother-in-law Paterne Berrichon, is from 19 December 1912 even though Gide mistakenly wrote 'November'. See André Gide, *Journal*, VOL. 1, *1887–1925* (Éric Marty ed.) (Paris: Gallimard, 'Bibliothèque de la Pléiade', 1996), pp. 742–3; for Marty's explanation of the corrected date, see p. 1594 n3.

*shit to God*!: Rimbaud reportedly carved 'Death to God' or 'Shit to God', depending on the narrative, into a Charleville park bench; see Whidden, *Rimbaud*, p. 32.

PAGE 37 | FOOTNOTES 19 and 20: Alain Borer's *Rimbaud in Abyssinia* is accurately cited.

*amputation of the leg*: That is, of course, what had actually happened; see Whidden, *Rimbaud*, p. 170.

PAGE 38 | *Rimbaud in 1921*. This photograph is of Abbot Joseph-Antoine Boullan (1824–93), a French priest who was accused of being an occultist and Satanist. In the last years of his life he befriended Joris-Karl Huysmans, who based the character of Dr Johannès from *Là-bas* (1891) on him. Despite Noguez's attribution, this portrait could not have been taken by Jean Roubier (1896–1981), who was born after Boullan's death. The photographer was particularly well known for images of his photojournalistic reports, during the interwar period, of writers at home. The correct attribution was first noted in Paul Léon, 'Images idiotes de Rimbaud', *Loxias* 27(1) (2009); available at: https://bit.ly/38j7Qyl [last accessed on 21 August 2021]. For more on Boullan and Huysmans, see Jules Bois, *Les Petites Religions de Paris* (Paris: Léon Chailley, 1894), pp. 120–30. The first major study that interpreted Rimbaud's poetry through the occult was by another abbot: Jacques Gengoux, *La Symbolique de Rimbaud: le système des sources* (Paris: La Colombe, 1947).

*November*: The novella was Flaubert's first completed work, written during the fall of 1842 and first published posthumously in 1910 in *Œuvres de jeunesses inédites*.

FOOTNOTE 21: Refers to fictitious works.

PAGE 42 | FOOTNOTE 22: Refers to a fictitious letter.

PAGE 43 | *abracadabratic vocabulary and images*: From 'The Drunken Boat'—'Devouring the green azures; where, like a pale elated / Piece of flotsam, a pensive drowned figure sometimes sinks'; 'And the yellow and blue awakening of singing phosphorus!' (*Complete Works*, p. 131); and the phrase 'syringes of the night' comes from *African Nights* (Chapter 4, p. 99).

'Abracadabratic' recalls the lines from the poem 'The Stolen Heart': 'O abracadabratic waves / Take my heart, let it be washed' (*Complete Works*, p. 73).

*the foam of things*: In fact, Valéry said that events, and not style, are the foam of things: 'Events are the foam of things. But *it is the sea that interests me*. It is in the sea that we fish; it is on her that we sail; it is into her that we dive . . . but foam? . . . .'—Paul Valéry, *Œuvres*, VOL. 2 (Jean Hytier ed.) (Paris: Gallimard, 'Bibliothèque de la Pléiade', 1960), p. 1508.

*the misanthrope of Fontenay*: Léautaud wrote his *Journal* while living in Fontenay-aux-Roses.

*Europe with its ancient parapets*: From 'The Drunken Boat' (*Complete Works*, p. 135).

*from Suez to the oasis of The Springs of Moses*: Refers to the Twelve Springs of Moses (spelt 'Oyun Musa', 'Uyun

Musa', 'Ayoun Moussa' or 'Ouyoon Moussa') in the Sinai Desert. According to legend, in December 1798 Napoleon Bonaparte saved his soldiers from the dangers of rising tides.

> On the 28th, he set out on horseback to go to Moses' Fountains. At three o'clock in the morning he crossed the Madieh, an arm of the sea three quarters of a league wide and crossable at low tide. Rear-Admiral Ganteaume mounted a gunboat, embarked sappers, engineers, several scientists, and went there by sea. Moses' Fountains are three leagues from Suez; there are nine of them. They are sources of water coming out of raised hillocks raised a few fathoms above the surface of the ground. They come from the mountains four leagues away.

—Napoléon Bonaparte, *Œuvres littéraires*, VOL. 4 (Tancrède Martel ed.) (Paris: Nouvelle librairie parisienne, 1888), pp. 230–3.

PAGE 44 | FOOTNOTE 23: No such publication exists. Noguez no doubt borrowed the name for its protagonist from the poet and philosopher Jacques Garelli (1931–2014), author of *Fragments d'un corps en archipel* suivi de *Perception et imaginaire: réflexions sur un poème oublié de Rimbaud* (2008). Both Garelli ('Boîte postale') and Noguez ('Etc. ou les silences du récit') contributed to Volume 8 of the literary journal *Revue Recueil*, entitled *Les Silences* (1988). Noguez likely also chose Garelli for the connection to Rimbaud that Aragon had established in the essay 'Garelli mis en pièces', the preface to a collection of several of Garelli's volumes of poetry; see Jacques Garelli, *De la création poétique; autour de l'œuvre de Jacques Garelli, préface et glose de Louis Aragon* (Paris: Éditions Encre marine, 2000). In a manner that recalls Jean Cocteau's foreword to Jean Desbordes's *J'adore* (see note on p. 83 in this volume), Aragon wrote:

> [W]e will find his words obscure and get angry ... and why not? Poetry is only clear after it sinks in. [. . .] I imagine the readers' faces, back in the day, if a newspaper of the Paris Commune had printed one of Arthur Rimbaud's *Illuminations*. That was nearly a century ago; since then, time has moved on, people have changed.

*written twenty years earlier*: Quotations from 'The Drunken Boat'—'Where, suddenly dyeing the blueness, delirium / And slow rhythms under the streaking of daylight, / Stronger than alcohol, vaster than our lyres / The bitter redness of love ferments!'; and 'I should have liked to show children those sunfish / Of the blue wave, the fish of gold, the singing fish.'

PAGE 45 | *attack of the Danakil warriors*: In February 1886, a Danakil tribe attacked and a travelling Frenchman and his wife, whose corpse was only identifiable by her gold tooth gleaming in the sun. See Carlo Zaghi, *Rimbaud in*

*Africa*: *con documenti inediti* (Naples: Guida editori, 1993), pp. 335–6, as cited in Graham Robb, *Rimbaud* (London: Picador, 2000), p. 364. Rimbaud narrowly escaped, although he confirmed that Danakils had held his caravan in Tadjourah for a year, and that they proceeded similarly with all travellers, only letting them go after stripping them of as much as they could. The lowest point in Africa, Lake Assal is a crater lake more than 150 metres below sea level, in the Danakil Desert, in central Djibouti. Dormant volcanoes and black lava fields surround its emerald water. Rimbaud lived near Lake Assal from late 1886 to early 1887, telling Alfred Bardey in August 1887 that its salt was inaccessible and unfit for sale; see Letter from Rimbaud to Bardey, 26 August 1887. Rimbaud describes the lake in his letter to the editor of the *Bosphore égyptien*, published on 25 and 27 August 1887:

> At six short stages of Tadjourah, about 60 kilometres, caravans descend to the salt lake by horrible roads reminiscent of the alleged horror of lunar landscapes. It seems that a French company is now being formed for the exploitation of this salt.
>
> Certainly, salt exists in very large areas, and perhaps quite deep, even though no soundings have been undertaken.

PAGE 46 | FOOTNOTE 24: All quotations are accurate; see *Complete Works*, pp. 327, 341 and 355, respectively.

PAGE 47 | *Voyage in Great Garabagnia*: This collection of Michaux's is part of a series of fictitious travel essays; see Henri Michaux, *Œuvres complètes*, VOL. 2 (Raymond Bellour and Ysé Tran eds) (Paris: Gallimard, 'Bibliothèque de la Pléiade', 2001), pp. 5–65.

FOOTNOTE 25: Refers to an article by Noguez in which he states that '*Voyage in Great Garabagnia* is one of the texts that contributed to the image of Michaux the humourist'—Dominique Noguez, 'Les voyages imaginaires de Michaux', *Liberté* 11 (6) (November-December 1969): 8.

PAGE 48 | FOOTNOTE 26: Bernard Frank wrote this passage in his review of a new edition of Nerval's *Œuvres complètes*, VOL. 2, which included *Le Voyage en Orient*, for Gallimard's 'Bibliothèque de la Pléiade' series. As Frank noted:

> This voyage is also an imaginary voyage. Whether in Malta, Egypt, Syria or Constantinople, Nerval seeks the remembrance of his lost *Je*. That expression is actually inadequate: in the Orient, he is looking for his dreams. He will verify, on the ground, what his head invents.'

For his part, in *Voyage en Orient* Nerval famously wrote: 'I travel to verify my dreams.' Oddly enough, Frank himself was the subject of a correction published in *Le Monde* on 24 December 1979 (in response to the confusion it had published on 14 and 18 December), entitled 'There Are At Least Three Bernard Franks.' Frank, the essayist who in 1979 was best known for his *Un siècle débordé*, which had received the 1971 Prix des Deux-Magots, had been confused with a Captain Poulailler (1887–1967) aka Bernard Frank, marine commander and author of studies of submarine stories; and with Bernard Frank the eminent Japanese scholar and translator of Fukuzawa, who had just been elected to the Collège de France. As the editors of *Le Monde* exclaimed: 'Poor Bernard Frank number two! First the Captain Poulailler sued him to get him to change his name (he had written under the pseudonym 'Bernard Frank' before the real Bernard Frank was even born!), then many novels, including *Un siècle débordé*, were attributed to another Bernard Frank, even though they had actually been written by him!'

PAGE 49 | *along the banks of the Marne*: Germaine Dulac (1882–1942), French filmmaker whose works include the *La Coquille et le Clergyman* (*The Seashell and the Clergyman*, 1928), based on Antonin Artaud's film scenario. She also made *La Fête espagnole* (*Spanish Fiesta*, 1920) and *Jour de fête* (*Celebration Day*, 1930), but not *Fête d'été*.

*Batcheff's bloody hands*: Pierre Batcheff (1907–32) is best known for his role in Luis Buñuel and Salvador Dalí's film *Un chien andalou* (*An Andalusian Dog*, 1929).

*demon of analogy*: A reference to Stéphane Mallarmé's prose work 'Le Démon de l'analogie'.

FOOTNOTE 27: Page 1013 of Antoine Adam's 1972 edition of Rimbaud's *Œuvres complètes*—which, for the real Rimbaud who died in 1891, is limited to one volume, and thus not numbered as such—is devoted to notes about prose poems, 'Historic Evening' and 'Bottom'.

A *lebdé* is a white wool cap, around which a handkerchief is tied to form a turban.

PAGE 50 | FOOTNOTE 28: As Noguez would later explain in 'Ressusciter Rimbaud' (p. 113–14), for this scene he does indeed draw on Achille Raffray, *Afrique orientale Abyssinie* (Paris: Plon, 1876), pp. 106–7. Noguez discovered Raffray in Alain Borer's *Rimbaud en Abyssinie* (Paris: Seuil, 1984); in English, *Rimbaud in Abyssinia* (Rosmarie Waldrop trans.) (New York: William Morrow, 1991). Noguez also adds Djami, Rimbaud's servant and companion during his later years; see Whidden, *Rimbaud*, p. 164.

PAGE 51 | FOOTNOTE 29: Yoshikazu Nakaji is the author of several important studies of *A Season in Hell*, including *Combat spiritual ou immense dérision? Essai d'analyse textuelle d'Une saison en enfer* (Paris: José Corti, 1987).

PAGE 52 | FOOTNOTE 30: While the publication exists, the pages cited do not: Lefebvre's *L'Image fascinante et le surréel* ends on page 285.

Quotation from *Water and Dreams*: Gaston Bachelard writes, 'Should we be surprised by children's enthusiasm for the tactile experience of pastes? Mrs Bonaparte recalled the psychoanalytic meaning of such an experience. Following psychoanalysts who isolated anal fixations, she recalls the interest, in young children and some neurotics, for their own excrement,' (Paris: José Corti, 1942, p. 148); and, in a note, he refers to Marie Bonaparte, *Edgar Poe* (Paris: Denoël et Steele, 1933), p. 457. Bachelard begins his next paragraph with: 'Silt is the dust of water, as ash is the dust of fire. Ash, silt, dust, and smoke produce images that change their matter endlessly. Through these diminished forms, elemental matter communicates. They are, in a way, the four dusts of the four elements. *Silt* is one of the most highly valued materials.' (pp. 148–9).

PAGE 53 | FOOTNOTE 31: Courtois actually wrote this passage about the line from the poem 'The Parisian Orgy; Or, Paris Is Repopulated': 'Here is the red-headed troupe of hip wrigglers' (*Complete Works*, p. 85).

FOOTNOTE 32: A fictitious essay, as Noguez knew all too well; he had joined the editorial board of the *Revue d'esthétique* in 1972, and became the editor-in-chief in 1978. Noémi Blumenkranz-Onimus' articles published in the journal include: 'La ville des futuristes', *Revue d'esthétique* 3–4 (1977): 73–104; and 'Les séminaires de M. Souriau,' in *Revue d'esthétique* 3–4 (1980): 269–72. A special issue edited by Noguez, entitled *Cinéma*:

*théorie, lectures*, was published in 1973, with a revised second edition appearing in 1978.

FOOTNOTE 33: A fictional reference.

PAGE 54 | FOOTNOTE 34: Noguez provides the French translation in the original—'Voici Arthur Rimbaud, le très lumineux explorateur des sanguinolentes nuits d'Afrique'.

PAGE 55 | FOOTNOTE 35: Noguez quotes from Roger Asselineau's French translation of Whitman's poems, published in 1972; the French lines that he provides in the original read:

> Foules d'hommes et de femmes [. . .]
>
> [. . .] les flammes qui sortent des cheminées
> de la fonderie; elles montent et flambent
> avec éclat dans la nuit [. . .]
>
> J'ai beaucoup aimé ces villes, beaucoup
> aimé ce fleuve majestueux et rapide . . .

PAGE 58 | *a little less Zang Tumb Tumb*: A poem written by Filippo Tommaso Marinetti and published in 1914, 'Zang Tumb Tumb' is a seminal modernist text, based on the Battle of Adrianople (November 1912–March 1913). Noguez would return to this poem in another story about Marinetti; see Dominique Noguez, 'Histoire en costume' in *Cadeaux de Noël: historiettes et maximes entrelardées de collages ou de dessins à feuilleter au moment des fêtes* (Paris: Zulma, 1998), p. 39.

FOOTNOTE 36: Noguez provides the French—'Pour l'amour de Dieu, ôtez-moi de là toute métaphysique! s'ils ont la vérité, qu'ils la gardent! [. . .] Allez ouste!'

PAGE 59 | Letter from Rimbaud to Thomas Mann: This fictitious letter refers to Mann's lecture 'Freud und die Zukunft' (Freud and the Future), which he delivered in Vienna on 8 May 1936, to commemorate Freud's eightieth birthday (as the honouree was ill and unable to attend, Mann travelled to Grinzing and read it to him in person the following month). See Thomas Mann, *Gesammelte Werke*, VOL. 9, *Reden und Aufsätze*, Part 1 (Frankfurt: Fischer, 1974), pp. 478–501. [I am grateful to Reinhard Pabst, Tim Trzaskalik, Rolf Bolt of the Thomas Mann Archives, Zürich, and Jim Reed for their assistance with locating these references.]

FOOTNOTE 37: Noguez provides the French 'La réaction en tant que progrès'. While it was never sent to Rimbaud, Thomas Mann did write the sentence in the 1929 essay: 'Reaktion als Fortschritt, der Fortschritt als Reaktion, diese Versch-ränktheit ist eine immer wiederkehrende geschicht-liche Erscheinung'—Reaction as progress, progress as reaction, this entanglement is a recurring historical phenomenon. See 'Die Stellung Freuds in der modernen Geistesgeschichte' in *Leiden und Größe der Meister* (Frankfurt: Fischer, 1982), pp. 885–95;

in English, 'Freud's Position in the History of Modern Thought' in *Past Masters and Other Essays* (H.T. Lowe-Porter trans.) (New York: Knopf, 1933), pp. 167–98; and in French, 'Freud dans l'histoire de la pensée moderne' in *Sur le mariage: Lessing, Freud et la pensée moderne* (Louise Servicen trans.) (Paris: Aubier-Flammarion, 1970), pp. 106–49.

Mann makes no mention of Rimbaud in Vienna in 1934. The phrase *Human, Too Human* is both the title of a book by Nietzsche (*Menschliches, Allzumenschliches I: Ein Buch für freie Geister*, 1878) and, as cinema scholar Noguez undoubtedly knew well, the title of a 1973 film by Louis Malle about an automotive plant.

FOOTNOTE 38: Thomas Mann portrayed Lodovico Settembrini as a representative figure of Italian humanism and, more generally, the Enlightenment.

*Messieurs Homais & Prudhomme*: In addition to being one of the nicknames that Verlaine gave Rimbaud (see Letter from Verlaine to Delahaye, 27 November 1875), the name 'Homais' more commonly refers to the apothecary in Gustave Flaubert's *Madame Bovary* who is characterized by his vanity and his narrow positivistic optimism.

Joseph Prudhomme is the archetypal French bourgeois who first appeared in Henry Monnier's drawings, stories and plays, and he was later the eponymous hero of a poem in Paul Verlaine's first collection, *Poèmes saturniens* (Poems Under Saturn), published in 1866.

FOOTNOTE 39: Noguez provides the French translation in the original—'On dansera ce soir!'

PAGE 61 | *interview with André Rousseaux*: A fictional reference, although Rousseaux published the essay 'La Vie aventureuse d'Arthur Rimbaud', *Revue universelle* 26(8): 225–32. Also, in the series 'Écrivains de nature', Rousseaux penned a long essay about Giono which appeared in *Le Figaro* on 26 December 1931 (p. 6) and 2 January 1932 (p. 6).

**PAGE 63** | *Mr Prudhomme was born with Christ*: Quoted from the poem 'The Impossible' (*Complete Works*, p. 297).

*the modern Ecclesiastes, namely,* Everyone: Quoted from 'Lightning' (*Complete Works*, p. 299).

*doesn't move fast enough*: Also, in 'Lightning', Rimbaud writes: 'What can I do? I understand what work is, and science moves too slowly' (*Complete Works*, p. 299).

*tied to loathed work*: Refers to the first line of 'Lightning', 'Work of man! this is the explosion which lights up my abyss from time to time' (*Complete Works*, p. 299).

**PAGE 64** | *a palimpsest on which earlier text is still visible*: This phrase draws on a passage from George Orwell's *1984*: 'All history was a palimpsest, scraped clean and reinscribed exactly as often as was necessary.'

FOOTNOTE 40: Noguez provides the French 'Chacun s'im-brique dans l'autre par un phénomène sans cesse renou-velé' in the footnote.

PAGE 65 | FOOTNOTE 41: The fictitious essay's reference to abortion (*avortée*) is a nod to Tertullian's famous oppo-sition to abortion from in *Apologeticum* 9, although he uses the verb *dissolvere*, to destroy, rather than a form of *delere*. Tertullian's use of words related to *deletus* most commonly denotes forgiveness (blotting out) of sins. [My thanks to Mark Edwards for his assistance with Tertullian.]

*Fondane in 1933*: See Benjamin Fondane, *Rimbaud le voyou* (Paris: Denoël & Steele, 1933), p. 23; reprinted by Éditions Complexe (1990), p. 43. Fondane wrote:

> We have to admit that with Rimbaud there is something new and wonderfully *efficient* in the world, that this spirit is, and in a frightful way, at the very centre of all our anxieties; that he *is perhaps the only one to ask for something that no one feels able to grant.*

PAGE 66 | '*alternating*' *à la Montherlant*: As Montherlant explained at the end of the preface to *Service inutile* (1935), borrowing Proudhon's motto from *Système des contradictions économiques ou philosophie de la misère* (1846): '*Ædificabo et destruam*—I will build and then I will destroy what I've built. An epigraph for this book, an epigraph for my life'—Henry de Montherlant, *Essais* (Pierre Sipriot ed.), (Paris: Gallimard, 'Bibliothèque de la Pléiade', 1963), p. 592. See also, Gerald Morreale, '"Alternance" and Montherlant's Aesthetics', *The French Review* 37(6) (May 1964): 626–36.

On *Saül*: About his first major play, written right after *The Fruits of the Earth* (*Nourritures terrestres*), Gide explained to pastor Eugène Ferrari in a letter (dated 15 March 1928) that: 'The dissolution of personality, to which a too-passive disposition to being receptive led, is the very subject of my *Saül* [. . .] which I wrote immediately after my *Nourritures*, as a kind of antidote or counterweight.'—André Gide, *Romans et récits. Œuvres lyriques et dramatiques*, VOL. 1 (Pierre Masson ed.) (Paris: Gallimard, 'Bibliothèque de la Pléiade', 2009), p. 1390.

FOOTNOTE 42: A fictional reference; Gide's journal entry begins from 29 September 1929 and makes no mention of Rimbaud in the text. See André Gide, *Journal*, VOL. 2 (Martine Sagaert ed.) (Paris: Gallimard, 'Bibliothèque de la Pléiade', 1997), pp. 145–6.

PAGE 67 | FOOTNOTES 43, 44 and 45: Refer to fictitious publications.

*fickle comings and goings between Sade and John* . . .: A fictitious quotation.

PAGE 68 | *the seismograph's movements*: Echoes both Aragon and Breton. Louis Aragon stated in an article: 'It is a fact that men have everything to learn from poets, and not poets as men but poets being poets. Poets are closer to the seismograph than they are to the citizen.'—see 'Introduction à 1930', *La Révolution surréaliste* 12 (15): 58. Towards the end of his novel *Nadja*, André Breton wrote: 'Beauty, neither dynamic nor static. The human heart, beautiful as a seismograph. Royalty of silence . . .' —see 'Nadja' in *Œuvres complètes*, VOL. 1 (Marguerite Bonnet ed.) (Paris: Gallimard, 'Bibliothèque de la Pléiade', 1988), p. 753.

PAGE 69 | *Boisdeffre's so ill-fitting phrase*: Pierre de Boisdeffre (1926–2002) was a writer and diplomat. When he was appointed French ambassador to Colombia, Bernard Frank wrote:

> One of the men who have scrutinized French literature from every possible angle for almost fifty years is unquestionably the ambassador of France [. . .], M. Pierre de Boisdeffre. [. . .] In the early '50s, it was a stylistic exercise popular among young writers to ridicule Boisdeffre. From [Roger] Nimier to your humble servant, countless are those took it up without any great danger.

—Bernard Frank, 'Notre ambassadeur à Bogota', *Le Monde*, 6 November 1985.

FOOTNOTE 46: Noguez quotes Rimbaud's letter verbatim.

PAGE 70 | FOOTNOTE 47: Refers to a fictitious essay, although Pieyre de Mandiargues' *Deuxième Belvédère* was published in 1962.

## List of Illustrations